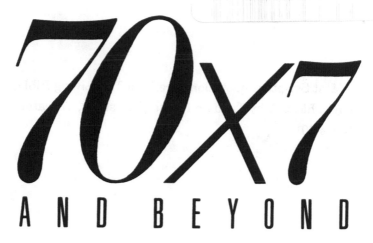

AND BEYOND

Monty Christensen
with Roberta
Lunsford Kehle

Prison Impact Ministries

ISBN 0-9618954-0-3

A Prison Impact Book

Cover Photograph by Chris Conrad

To Jack and Adel Rozell
for their continued Christ-like example

CONTENTS

UP FRONT

When the going gets tough—run. Until a few years ago that injunction fit Holly and me. It's S.O.P. (Standard Operating Procedure) for a lot of people—those unhappy in their marriage and contemplating divorce, street kids, and especially for those people who keep prison doors revolving. Three-fourths of the boys with whom I was in reform school, I saw as men in prison.

Examining old memories has been painful, but we pray that by sharing them, even one reader will stop running and allow the Holy Spirit to begin the healing process. And if our experiences help those who deal with people coming out of bondage, we are grateful.

Names and identities of some of the persons in this book have been changed in order to protect their privacy.

I am aware that there are dedicated, conscientious workers in many different institutions, and different opportunities for help. I can only tell what happened to me.

My collaborator, Roberta Kehle, and I deeply appreciate the number of people who gave time and talents to this manuscript, especially Myrtle Batchelor, Aletha Campbell, and Beverly Emery, for typing and proofreading, and Jeff Boetcher for the cover design. Thanks go to Roma Tunberg and the other prayer warriors who prayed the book into being.

But most of all, my grateful thanks to my precious Holly.

Monty Christensen
June, 1987

70 X 7

AND BEYOND

Monty Christensen
with Roberta
Lunsford Kehle

Prison Impact Ministries

1

Cocaine, a Cadillac, and a Thirty-eight Special

The mountain pass highway out of Missoula descended fast after the summit, as though it couldn't wait to get me out of Montana. It deposited me in Grangeville, Idaho, at one o'clock on a warm June morning in 1976.

Along quiet streets, four-way blinker stoplights reflected in the windows of lifeless, one-story buildings. The movie theatre's marquee announced *Smokey And The Bandit*, but missing bulbs gave it a chicken-pox appearance. Several people in their early twenties, my bracket, crowded out of the theatre's double doors and headed for a pickup truck.

I lowered my window. "Which way to Portland, Oregon?"

"Go right, through Lewiston," one of them yelled. He surveyed my yellow 'seventy-three Eldorado. "Nice wheels. Hey! Want to party? We've got beer."

I followed them to a house where a party was in progress, and introduced myself as Monty Montana.

To show my appreciation for their hospitality, I opened my attache case and broke out cocaine and Thai sticks. I stuffed my thirty-eight special in my jacket.

"Man, that's a lot of dope," someone said. "You get busted and you've had it."

I blew him away. "I'd rather die than let a cop take me, and I'll kill any cop who tries!"

There was a murmur of mixed approval and awe. Even in my drug stupor I realized they sized me up as a heavy trafficker. Who else would blow into town with a three-year-old Cadillac, lots of dope and a gun? Let them think it. I had left a trail of so many lies and half-truths, one more wouldn't hurt.

Everyone wanted to buy stuff, and I had plenty. Besides, I needed cash to get to Oregon and to Uncle Truman, the only one who could help me. So the next day when a guy who was up on the dopers said he knew a place in Lewiston where both of us could sell stuff, I said, "Let's go."

We parked my Caddy in the driveway and jumped in his jazzed up 'fifty-six Plymouth drag car with a 426 Hemi. Attracted attention like blazes, but the guy's parents were important in town, so the cops probably left him alone. Not exactly like Monty "Montana" Christensen.

I snugged the guy's pot stash under the seat and leaned back, remembering the judge who said, "I see no reason Monty need go to the reform school. Who will take custody of him?"

And no one stepped forward. Not Mom, not Grandma. My stepdad, forget it, and my real dad didn't know about the problem. I went to reform school by default.

We cut around a produce truck while the Plymouth driver slapped his hand to a rock song. I braced my feet and looked at him. Some of us were born on the right side of town.

The Lewiston contact wasn't there. We got something to eat and got back to Grangeville about midnight. I wished we had made the trip in the Eldorado so I could let this guy off and go on my way. A bad feeling started in my stomach, and it wasn't from the fifth of wine I had with dinner. Something was up.

We stopped in front of the house. My car sat in the driveway, but the bad gut feeling was still with me. I touched the bulge under my jacket where the gun rested in my belt.

"You go in," I said. "Leave the motor running."

"Sure, Montana. But it looks quiet. Got the coke on you?"

"In my pocket."

"Okay." He laughed. "Just don't run off with my stash."

He went into the house. The faint grumble of a gearing down semi coming off the pass drifted through the open car window.

Then fast as a diamondback rattler on its tail can

3

strike, two guys in jeans and plaid shirts burst out of the front door and ran for the car. One braced an automatic, and light bounced off the other's shotgun.

I had been set up. Those so called "nice people" were ripping me off. They would get my money and the couple ounces of coke I had left. I would be stranded.

I slid to the driver's seat, but they were at the car, shoving the shotgun in one window and the automatic in the other. Straight at my head.

"Freeze! Police!"

My insides turned to liquid. Police! Possession and intent to deliver were both thirty years in Idaho. Sixty years. Not to mention priors.

I lay over in the seat, punched "Drive" on the push button transmission, and jammed my foot down on the gas pedal. The car shot forward, and I grabbed the steering wheel with one hand trying to peer over the dashboard.

Pop, pop, pop. They were shooting at the car. Then boom—boom. The shotgun went off.

The car shimmied hard with a rupturing screech. The flat from the detonated tires sounded like tarps in the wind. I hung on, the steering wheel slippery in my sweaty hands. Rocks from the downhill gravel road machine-gunned the fenders, and the smell of burning rubber filled the inside of the car.

Dead ahead another gravel road intersected. The Plymouth's nose hit the ground and bounced into

4

weightlessness as it flew through the air.

My throat was like a wound-up rubber band. I fumbled for my gun, but it dropped when we nose-dived. I gripped the steering wheel with one hand, got the coke with the other, and in mid-air threw the incriminating evidence out the passenger window.

The next instant my body whiplashed as the car smashed to the ground, slid sideways and spun twice, then slammed against the curb and stopped.

"Get out of the car, Monty!" I yelled at myself. "Get out of the car!"

Coke and adrenalin combined forces, and my body seemed on the verge of exploding. I grabbed the door handle on the driver's side and pulled. It broke off in my hand.

The police were maybe a block-and-a-half away. Where was the gun? I couldn't find it. My heart felt huge, as if there were nothing else in my body except its enormous pounding. I crawled out the passenger door and sprinted.

"Stop! Police!" They shouted at me, but I kept running. Halfway through a big field I dropped to my hands and knees in the tall wet alfalfa, and crawled. I couldn't see where I was going. I ran into a barbed wire fence, climbed through and kept on.

To my right, the porchlight on a trailer house illuminated a fat man with a rifle running out the door. He froze at the yell, "Police! You're under arrest!"

I crouched down, biting at the wire cuts in my hand, and watched in disbelief as the cops had this poor guy on his face. He must have heard the shooting and noise, and thought he was under attack, so flew out of his house with his gun—and the cops thought it was me.

That guy doesn't know how lucky he is they didn't kill him, I thought. I wished I could tell him I was sorry. I needed to tell a lot of people. Holly and Jared were at the top of the list. Then Uncle Truman who had believed in me. And Grandma. The Caddy wasn't worth it.

A police car screamed up to the trailer, and a voice rang, "You idiots! The guy we want is six feet tall and slender. You think this guy's it? Spread out and find the right one!"

I crawled away praying the dark would wrap around me.

* * *

PARADISE TRAILER COURT — The softly lighted sign sent a faint buzz into the court's quiet darkness. But it wouldn't be quiet for long.

An old bus converted into a camper sat apart from the nicer trailers. I looked hard at the double doors. They were ajar. I pushed them gently. Was someone there? Every blood vessel in my body seemed to bulge from terror and drugs.

The doors opened and I listened. No sounds. I eased up the steps, pulled the door back, and locked it. I crept to the back. A pile of clothes lay beneath one of the bunks. I crawled under, pulled the clothes on top of me, and lay shaking.

It didn't take long for the action to start. Sirens shrilled into the court. The bus's thinly curtained windows couldn't deflect the police car's red-and-blue lights flashing like whizzing gum balls. Floodlights glared and radios crackled instructions in high static to searchers who called to each other.

I tried to stop trembling and not to breathe as I heard the bus doors rattle. "It's locked," someone said. I heard them poking around under me.

Car engines gunned, and the occupants of other trailers yelled, "What's going on?"

By degrees my body settled down under the hot, stuffy clothes. They must have looked for me for several hours.

One by one the lights dissipated, and the cars left. I pushed aside a smelly blanket, and turned on a small radio. Maybe there was information about the chase.

No news, and middle-of-the-night disc jockeys don't talk much. This one rolled Jim Croche singing "Time in a Bottle." That had been a favorite at the Jekyll and Hyde Bar in Billings where Holly and I met. Beautiful blue-eyed Holly...no, hazel eyes set in a face as smooth and clear as a Montana spring morning. God, I missed her. The song lyrics reached

7

out to grab me.

> If I could put time in a bottle,
> The first thing I would do, would be
> Save everyday
> Til eternity passes away—
> And spend it all with you.

I groaned, and the groan echoed in my ears as though from a bottomless grave. Oh, to imprison the time with Uncle Truman and afterward with Holly. To breathe its fragrance, sip its sweetness—the first time my life meant something, when it counted.

But I would pour out the times that I screamed as an evil force tried to suck me into itself.

I would pour out all the days I didn't want to remember. Beginning with the Tonka trucks....

2

Beginnings

1959

"I want Mom!" My six-year-old insides heaved with furious sobs at the man who recently married my mother.

He had hit me on the side of the head because I reached in front of him for the jelly at the breakfast table.

"You're in first grade. Ought to know better!"

My ear and cheek burning, I ran from the trailer house to our Montana sage-frosted backyard.

The ol' guy slapped me a lot. Mom said he had a mean temper. Sometimes she'd try to stop him, and then they would fight.

In the dust, grasshoppers jumped around my beloved Tonka trucks. Everyday I spent hours making bulldozer sounds and scooping dirt for roads and towns. The trucks were special like Mom, but the anger and pain inside me screamed for release. With running eyes and nose, I smashed them.

When Mom got home from her job at the truck-stop diner, he got to her first. "Shirley, that kid of yours hasn't got any manners. He needs to be taught a few things."

Mom wearily nodded her head. I tiptoed outside and forced the pooling tears back in my eyes.

It didn't take long to catch on that my stepfather and I were in a contest for Mom, and he was winning. He either ridiculed me in front of her or physically knocked me around. To escape as much as possible, I ran to my grandparents' gas station and watched them pump gas.

After a couple of hours Grandpa said, "Break!" and we'd go to their house. From the refrigerator he'd get a beer and take a long swig.

"Mmmm. I was thirsty."

At lunchtime he had another beer with his bologna sandwich. For the afternoon break, another.

"Mmmm, good, huh, Grandpa?"

"Sure is, m'boy. Helps me deal with problems. Want a sip?"

It was bitey and sour, but I couldn't wait to be big to drink it.

Whenever Mom went to Grandma's house, Grandma lit into her.

"Shirley, you and that husband of yours aren't treatin' Monty right. He comes here with bruises on him like I've never seen. Yet the girl gets by with murder."

From the other room I heard Mom mumble something.

"Don't 'Ma' me," Grandma flared. "Seems like with Monty you're holding a mirror but don't want to look at yourself. Don't want to touch that part of you. I know he came of a bad marriage, and reminds you of your first husband, but that's not Monty's fault."

I wasn't sure what it was about, but I got a tingly feeling. Grandma was sticking up for me. No one ever did that.

After the visits Mom told my stepdad what Grandma had said.

"That's none of her business!" he'd yell. "Tell her to quit interfering. And tell your kid not to go over there."

But when I couldn't handle life I ran—to Grandma's or anywhere. My folks would call the police. After a few repeats, someone decided that since I had trouble staying home, I should be placed with another family.

I was ten years old and didn't want to stay with strangers. I didn't want fences. As bad as the abuse was at home, I wanted Mom and the familiarity of home life. I ran from each receiving home.

Next the judge told us to get counseling. Mom and I went downtown to a big building. A lady in an office put her hand on my head.

"Monty needs firm guidelines, but needs the security to be able to show his emotions without fear of punishment. He needs to make mistakes without being ridiculed."

I didn't understand, but guess Mom did. She must have told my stepdad, because for awhile he didn't lose his temper or ridicule me in front of others as much as before. Slowly, the scared, numb feeling, so long a part of me, left. Maybe I could laugh or cry without being punished. Maybe I was loved.

Several weeks before Christmas as we sat at the dinner table, my stepsister spooned more macaroni and cheese on her plate and announced, "I wrote a letter to Santa today and asked him for a Barbie doll and some new skates. Do you think he'll bring them?"

My stepdad winked at Mom. "Well, I wouldn't be surprised. He likes little girls."

My heart skipped faster. Months before I never would have confided to them what my long-time dream was, but things were different. I'd do it.

"You know, all the guys in my fifth grade have bikes. My friend's dad got him a neat one from the auction. Hardly cost anything. Sure would be great havin' a bike." I was too big to believe in Santa Claus. I knew where presents came from.

"Think you could ever learn how to ride one?" My

stepdad snickered and kept eating.

Well, at least he hadn't said no. For the next few weeks, just thinking about bikes and popping wheelies made me so excited I couldn't take a deep breath.

Christmas morning I tiptoed across cold floors to peek in the living room. The Christmas tree breathed its piney scent into the room's chill. Bright packages covered the white tissue paper around the tree's base. No bicycle. They had hidden it. I crept back to bed, shivering more from excitement than the cold.

When it was time for presents, my sister tried out her new skates in the living room and squealed with delight at the Barbie and wardrobe. I waited. My turn was coming.

Here it came. "And for Monty...this."

I looked down. "This" was one of the fire trucks you could get with a fill-up at the gas station. I tried to swallow the heaviness in my throat, but it wouldn't go down.

Nobody said anything. They didn't have to. Inside I knew this was my stepdad's way of making me understand my place in the family. I hated his guts, but didn't dare cry or show him how much I hated him.

I received another present—warm socks from Grandma—but they didn't dissipate the rejection, the overwhelming feeling of aloneness. My teeth bit through the skin inside my lower lip. I didn't look at anyone or the ugly tree as I went to the bathroom to unleash hot tears.

That Christmas signaled the end of the respite and the beginning of my understanding that things would always be this way. Or worse.

A couple of months later I ran home with a squirming brown-and-white puppy in my arms. A friend had given me one from his new litter. My first pet. I hadn't stopped to think what my stepfather would say. He didn't like anything going on that he didn't control.

I was later than usual because the choosing took time. Wedging the puppy between chin and arms, I opened the door. The only thing I saw was a fist coming at my face.

"I'll teach you to be late."

The blow hit below my eye and I staggered back. The puppy jumped to the ground and fled through the open door while my stepfather jerked me inside and smashed his other fist into my stomach, knocking me into a corner. I couldn't breathe. This was worse than his other beatings.

Gasping, I pleaded, "What did I do?"

"My rule is, you don't come home late. Seen you through the window, tryin' to sneak that dog in here before you asked me about it."

His boot crunched into my side. I tried to curl into a ball and use my arms as shields from the kicks.

When he spent his outburst, I lay for a couple of minutes, then licked my lips, tasting salt and the rusty taste of blood. I wiped my sleeve across the mess. It stung. Bad.

"Get that dog back where he came from," my stepfather ordered.

I found the puppy and carried the comforting bundle back to my friend's house. "It's okay," I said, my chin on the warm head. "Don't feel bad. You're going to your mom. She'll take care of you." I hugged the puppy tighter. "Wish I were you."

* * *

With a start my mind came back to the present. Gray light forced its way around the curtains of the old bus, sweeping through my thoughts of my childhood. My watch showed almost six o'clock. I peeked through the curtains. The trailer court sign had been turned off and the court still slumbered under the murkey dawn.

Last night seemed like a dream. The car flying through the air, the flashing lights, shots aimed at me. It couldn't have been real, but I knew it was and that I had to get out of there. The police would be back.

I rummaged through the old clothes strewn around the bus, looking for a disguise. I pulled a pair of greasy coveralls over my own clothes and wadded junk in a paper sack to make it look like a lunch sack. A crescent wrench lay on the floor near the driver's seat. I stuffed it in my back pocket, and eased out of the bus and the court—just an ordinary working stiff on his way to the job.

The first few minutes' elation at having made it thudded to the black-topped road under my feet. Where was I going? Walking along the highway with an A.P.B. out on me, I might as well be wearing a sign, "HEY, COPS, PICK ME UP." Besides, I couldn't walk to Oregon.

A whiff of frying bacon elbowed into my worries. The aroma came from a nearby park where tents and campers braided through scrub pine trees. One group, bicyclists, were stowing gear in a red pickup. I walked over to two young women, who were climbing in.

"Hey," I said, crossing my fingers that they hadn't heard any news reports, "my car broke down. Could you give me a ride up the road so I can get a mechanic to fix it?"

We drove about a mile when we pulled into a restaurant's parking lot.

"We're all stopping here for breakfast," they said. "You come too, and then we'll take you to the next town."

I didn't dare go into a place around Grangeville. I stammered the first thing that came to my mind. "Oh, no, that's okay. I...uh...don't feel all right. Couldn't eat a thing...really, not a thing." To prove my point, as soon as they were out of the truck, I plopped over on the seat.

I lay there awhile trying to figure my move. At the next place, should I call Holly or hop a bus to Portland and Uncle Truman? I needed help more than ever. The thought of turning myself in didn't occur to me. Running was the way I did things.

Whatever I did, I could use this time to freshen up. I wouldn't be noticed if I sidled into the restaurant's washroom and right back.

My drivers waved to me from their window seat. The restaurant was filled. Glad I hadn't gone in.

We started on our way and about three minutes down the road, cop cars from nowhere swarmed around us with sirens going, lights flashing. Highway patrols, three sheriffs' and a couple unmarked. How had they known?

"Oooh, what did I do? I wasn't speeding. Honest, I wasn't speeding!" The truck driver swerved to a stop on the shoulder and looked at her companion and me, begging us to believe her.

I laughed. "Somehow, I don't think we're going to get a speeding ticket."

In a flash we were surrounded by a score of police pointing shot guns at us from behind open car doors. One of the officers pulled an electronic bull horn from his car. I nearly laughed again. This was big stuff— a drug dealer, a Cadillac, the big shoot-out. They were after bad dude Monty Montana.

The girls in the pickup were so scared they were crying. I felt bad. "Don't worry about it," I said. "They're after me."

One girl started to get out of the cab, and a voice shot through the loudspeaker. "You! Crawl on your stomach. Get out and lie flat on your face and don't move!"

The girls really freaked out. Screaming and crying. I got out and walked around the back of the truck. If it hadn't been for the fact that my system was still loaded with drugs, I wouldn't have had the guts to do it.

But the drugs expressed my relief that the chase was over. I put my hands in the air and, laughing like a hyena, walked toward the shotguns and pistols.

For a few seconds there was confusion.

"What's Montana doing?" someone yelled.

"Watch it, he may have a bomb!"

The confusion didn't last long, and the next thing I knew they rushed me and pushed my face into the highway. Someone yanked back my arms and I felt metal bands tighten and grate against my wrists while I was frisked and leaned against a cop car. They believed the girls' hysterical story and sent them on their way.

I couldn't stop laughing. The whole scene was funny. I laughed all the way to jail.

* * *

I was running, chased by ghostly figures angry with me because I couldn't do what they wanted. I hit a bump and flew into the air. I flapped my arms and kicked my legs. I had to keep going, but I was so tired. Push, Monty, push. Slower, slower.

My stepfather's face appeared. "I told you you couldn't learn to ride a bike!"

I felt myself sinking to the ground. My stepfather's boot was there—waiting for me. It kicked me in the stomach. I felt sick. I had to throw up.

I snapped out of my nightmare and barely made it to the jail's latrine. Drying out was never easy. For the next day, drug demons tormented me in nightmares. Awake, they racked my mind with memories, and marched past all the sins I had ever committed.

My life flicked before me like a fast-card shuffle. Almost all of it dealing with my rejection.

* * *

After the beating I received bringing home the puppy, I had stayed away from my stepfather as much as possible, which meant staying away from home. Most of the time he didn't care and Mom seemed relieved because then there were no problems.

Kids my age were home with their parents, so I hung around with older boys, fourteen and fifteen.

One night when we finished looking at the magazines in the grocery store, we went outside and passed around cigarettes. I was just learning to inhale without coughing and glanced down to make sure I was fingering the cig the right way.

"We need beer money," one of the guys said. "Kid, wanna help?"

"Sure," I said, following them down the road.

A car sat under a burned-out street light. "You're our look-out, kid. Tell us if anyone comes."

I was scared, but wanted the guys to accept me. In a minute one of them pulled something from under the hood, and we ran back up the street.

The next time, I watched how they unwired the battery, and the time after that, I did it myself. I knew we shouldn't do these things, but each time I lifted a battery or stole a radiator and sold it, it got easier.

None of us ever went to church. My stepdad didn't like the preachers telling him what he could and couldn't do. At least that's what he said they did. And he sure didn't like their asking for money. It was fun watching the games Mom and he played with them.

One day the new preacher in town came by the house. They intercepted him in the driveway.

"Nice to meet you, Reverend. We've been meanin' to get the kids to Sunday School. What time does it start? Oh, yes, well, if we can.... By the way, Reverend." My stepfather could barely suppress a smirk as he tossed his favorite question. "How does your church feel about the pool halls and whore houses? Bad people down there. Goin' to run 'em out of town?"

That question most always got the reverends flustered. They'd either figure here was a moral kindred spirit and would outline their plans to rid Billings of such influences, or they would leave fast. Either way, my stepfather enjoyed imitating them before an audience.

This minister looked my stepfather in the eye. "Those people need to know about God's love, that He forgives seventy times seven and more. He loves us all that much. Including you, Sir. Come to church and hear more about it."

As the preacher walked away, my stepfather opened and closed his mouth, but didn't say anything. I stood there trying to figure out how much seventy times seven was. I got a stick and made marks in the dirt. Four hundred ninety times. Wow! And more besides that. Why would anyone need to be forgiven that much?

* * *

Our family went wherever work was. The year I was thirteen we moved to the Red Lodge area, nearly on the Yellowstone Park border. Giant snow-capped Granite Peak dominated the horizon, reminding humans of their size.

Our job was to tear down an old three-story school, brick by brick. My chore was to clean off the mortar. Years later I could feel the grit caked into the pores of my hands and smell the suffocating powder kicked up by the wire brush.

But at a penny each, I could clean four to five hundred bricks a day, unless my sister and I got in a fight. When she made me mad, I could clean seven hundred.

With the money, I bought a minibike. It didn't run, and I welcomed help from a kid who was a good mechanic. He rebuilt the engine and didn't charge me a cent.

He also took me into the high country to rabbit hunt or trap. When the dirt roads were packed with snow, we'd get an old car hood and talk someone into pulling us around with their truck. We'd tie the hood on the back of the pickup, throw blankets in it and hang on, careening twenty to thirty miles an hour along the roads. In hot weather, we floated down the irrigation ditches and down the big, winding wood sloughs.

The guy was a good friend, but strange. He talked about God as if he knew Him and even liked Him.

"Come to church with me, Monty."

"Nah," I replied, mimicking my stepdad. "I can get along without religion." I laughed, trying to sound important. "Besides, I've done pretty bad stuff."

"That doesn't make any difference. God loves you and forgives a lot."

There was that word—forgives. Funny how it had stuck in my mind. I heard my voice sound rough. "Oh, yeah? Like four hundred ninety times?"

He looked puzzled. "What?"

"Never mind. Let's get out the twenty-two and go shoot cans."

We lived there one year. Each morning at five-thirty I shivered my way out of bed on the unheated porch, and stoked kindling in the old trash burner. I thought about the rest of the family peacefully sleeping in the house. There was room for me inside, but out here was "my place." Why? Why was my life so different from that of other kids—so hard? It was like someone drew straws, and I got the short one. At thirteen, the vines of anger and bitterness already had a squeeze-hold on me. How could I handle it? I ran.

* * *

"Monty, your junior high principal called. Said you've been skipping school. Said you hang out with the wrong kind of kids. Why are you doing this to me? I'm tired after working twelve hours a day. I don't want to hear this."

We were back in Billings, and I wasn't surprised

that someone called Mom, just mad that she was coming down on me. I decided to work an angle.

"Mom, let me go live with Dad. Things will be okay then. Tell me where he is."

She put me on the bus for Utah. Dad had a Mormon wife, and enrolled me in a Mormon school. I learned about Mormon rules. No cokes, no coffee. But I would stick it out—make Dad love me and be proud of me.

To get acquainted, the two of us went deer hunting for a couple of days. My very own dad and the crisp mountain air. The feeling of being a son hesitantly touched me, then settled in a warm glow.

When we returned from the trip, Dad's new wife didn't smile, and said not a word as she served dinner. That night I heard them arguing. The next day Dad came in my room and stood rubbing his chin.

"Monty, there's...ah...a problem you'd better know about. Your stepmother is upset. Says I love you more than her. And...ah...she wants you to leave. I'm really sorry, Monty, but...you understand. You'll have to go back to your mother. I'm really sorry, Monty."

There didn't seem to be any long straws in the bunch. For me, anyway.

* * *

In Billings, life picked up where I left it. At home I dodged fists, and at school I was too shy to get into sports or other activities.

"Hear about Christensen?" the guys I hung around with cracked up one afternoon. "He gets his girl a necklace and is so chicken he just drops it in front of her and splits. Ha! Ha! Here, Christensen, have a beer. Make ya feel more like a man."

The beer and pot someone passed around did their tricks. I laughed and spaced out. The guys were right. I liked myself after a few beers, so keggers became my big thing. I got good at forging my mother's name on excuses to cut school. But I didn't feel there was anything wrong with that. My stepfather had taught me to get it over on people.

"The punk at the gas station forgot to charge for the oil," he'd say, or "I really suckered the store on that deal. Those big guys will stick it to you, so you gotta get 'em first."

Therefore, school was a chance to get over on authority. My parents wouldn't let me grow my hair over my ears, but at lunchtime we'd roll our T-shirt sleeves and go off campus to smoke or swig from a bottle of 190-proof alcohol someone brought.

One day my science class examined a snake in a jar. "Don't disturb him," the teacher warned.

When they passed the snake to me, I shook him a little. A blackboard eraser hit my head. The teacher yanked me out in the hall and slammed me against the lockers.

"I've had it with you, Christensen. Down to the principal's office."

The principal hit his palm against the desk. "Monty, what's your problem? You're out of school a lot, you're not handing in you work—and now disobedience. I'm calling your parents."

When I got home, my stepfather cussed, and hit me so hard I tasted blood. I bolted through the door. I would never come back, but a couple of days later, after crashing at someone's house, the cops slapped me in jail for running away. Coming to retrieve me, my stepdad belted me twice as hard.

"Look at your sister," he yelled. "She's no trouble. Everyone likes her. And I don't get called to the jail for your stepbrother."

Well, I couldn't be like my sister. She was accepted by everyone, including the family. My stepbrother, six years older than I, didn't live at home, but his dad had no idea what an influence he was on me. He was my booze supplier. Every time I determined to stay out of trouble, he'd approach me with beer, and want me to sell it at school. I didn't have the guts to stand up to him.

So the cycle of running and jail repeated, and disgorged me in front of the county juvenile judge.

I looked up at the high desk, and farther up at the black-robed figure. My knees shook.

The judge read my reports. "This boy is only in junior high school. He's done nothing to warrant sending him to reform school."

My stepfather had held that possibility over my head. I breathed a sigh of relief.

The judge peered over at me. "We'll try the state mental hospital."

3

The Chains Tighten

I was the youngest patient in the hospital and scared out of my wits. Nights I awakened in terror to blood-curdling screams. I never knew where they came from, but they were always followed by heavy footsteps and silence.

In the ward's dayroom, old guys stared at me, followed my every move through eyes that never seemed to blink. Some of them would laugh for hours at a time in a weird rhythm. Some smashed furniture.

The doctors told me that whatever was wrong with me would show in the tests they gave me, but they never seemed to find out anything. They wouldn't release me because I had nowhere to go. Mom didn't want me back home.

No one ever came to see me, but another patient had a lot of visits from a guy from Butte, Montana. When he came, he always took time to talk to me. When he heard my problem, he said, "Tell the judge

I'll be your temporary guardian. Stay with me until you get your problems straightened out."

The judge okayed the idea, and the guy drove me to Butte. We went out for pizza. This wouldn't be bad.

"Here we are," he said, opening the door to his house.

We stepped inside, and he put his arms around me and nuzzled my face. His scalding breath whispered suggestions in my ear.

My heart did a flipflop. Whoa! What was this? A queer!

"Get out of here, you stinkin' pervert!" I yelled.

"No, you get out of here if you don't like it."

I did. Out the door, hitched back to Billings, and got arrested for parole violation.

"Judge," I pleaded, "the guy's a queer. I didn't want to stay with him."

The judge seemed a long way away, as though he were sitting on top of the world, and I was a scoop of dirt he needed to dump someplace. Just like me with my old Tonka trucks.

He cleared his throat. "I don't know what to do with you. Your mother doesn't want the responsibility of keeping you in line, and no one else has offered. Reform school is the only answer. I'm sorry, Son. I'm really sorry."

He could tell me ten times he was sorry. Seventy

times—four hundred ninety times. Everyone said they were sorry. No one ever meant what they said.

* * *

"Christensen, we've got three phases here." The reform school's supervisor leaned his elbows on his desk and wagged a pencil at me. "You behave yourself, you'll make the third. If not, you'll wish you had."

I hated walls and closed-in feelings. I was scared. I was homesick. I wanted out of there, and I knew the only way out was to toe the mark. For the next few weeks I followed the rules and did everything they told me.

Early on, my counselor had said, "Monty, I'm your friend. If I'm to help you, you have to trust me."

I relaxed, and little by little, opened my thoughts and feelings of rejection to him.

One day he said, "You've earned a weekend furlough. Where do you want to spend it?"

I shrugged. "I don't know. Mom doesn't want me. Maybe I'll stay here."

"Tell you what," he said, "come to my house. That's better than staring at your cell walls."

We were barely inside his door when he handed me a bottle of beer and hashish. I had never had hashish before, but what do you do?

We ate sunflower seeds and got loaded on hash-ish. About the time I began getting nauseous signals from my stomach, he made his move on me. I ran from the other fag, but although I struggled now, this one had my thin arm in vise grips.

"You'd better go along with me, Monty," he said in a soothing tone. "I could put you in violation. You know that means an added sentence."

I was panic-stricken. He was so strong.

But at that moment, my salvation queased into my stomach. As the mound of sunflower-seed shells grew higher, so did the waves of nausea. I barfed all over him.

He immediately took me back to the school, giving heavy insinuations about what would happen to me if I told. Lying on my cot, I shook with revulsion. Although he hadn't done anything, I still felt dirty, and I couldn't tell anyone what had happened. Be-sides his threats, no one would believe me. After all, he was part of an administration. The system. My stepfather had drilled into my head that the system is the enemy. And it just proved itself.

I knew only one way to handle it—the thing I did best. I ran.

It didn't take long for the authorities to find me and bring me back by the scruff of the neck. They took me to a solitary concrete cell hole.

"Keep the blanket spread tight on your cot. An' stay off it," the guard barked.

I dropped my few belongings, and after he was gone, stretched out on the cot and closed my eyes.

"Off that bed!" The guard stood in the doorway. "Mebbe standing on the wall will help you remember rules!"

He motioned me out in the hall and stood me about eight inches from the wall. "Hands behind your back," he spat. "Now, stand there and don't move 'til I tell ya." He walked a few feet away and straddled a chair, never taking his eyes from me.

After a few minutes the mucky-colored wall blurred. My knees locked but I dared not move them. From the corner of my eye I saw the guard pour coffee from a thermos. The sound of tramping feet meant guys heading for lunch. The guard took a sandwich from his lunch box. Over an hour must have gone by. I couldn't feel my legs. They felt like stumps.

The tramping feet again. The guys going back to their cells. Another hour had passed. Still I stood. I was sick to my stomach. My head felt like swirling snow. Black dots floated in front of my eyes. As I felt myself buckling, the guard pushed me.

"Back to your cell. Don't let me catch you on that bed again."

Twenty-eight days in solitary went by with no visitors. The only thing there was to do was dribble water on my daily vitamin and watch the pill expand. Sometimes my throat ached as though tears had piled up halfway and couldn't get out. I'd jam my pillow over my face and let them escape.

Mom came to see me once in the eleven months I was in reform school. That one visit made the rest of the sentence almost bearable.

I tried to balance on the rope of keeping distance between the counselor and me, and not angering him. A lot for a fourteen year old.

Every week the counselor had night therapy sessions. Our "therapy" was to "go out of ourselves." To connect with another world. He made a couple of guys his helpers. They placed a black rug in the center of the room and put a candle in the middle.

I sat in the back of the room and inched closer to the door. I didn't like this stuff.

When the candle was removed, we were supposed to imagine a deep hole, a pit, and things rising from it. The air was oppressive. My skin crawled. I didn't know the terms, but knew this was getting to the basis of something bad.

The two guys who were the helpers both died shortly after getting out of reform school. One was in a car accident and the other, in what was called a hunting accident. Both deaths were seemingly unrelated to each other, but it was as though the master of the alien territory they had trespassed demanded their lives. An unsettling thought hit me. Maybe he wanted me, too.

* * *

"It's good to see you, Monty," Mom greeted me.

"What are your summer plans?"

The sentence was over and someone from the state took me home. It was the spring of 1969, the summer before my tenth grade.

Mom really did seem glad to see me, but it was plain she was worried about what trouble I'd get into next. The thing was, I was so glad to be home, I was determined to stay out of trouble. I tried to exude confidence.

"I've got that planned, Mom. I want to get away from the old friends and see new country, so think I'll head north to Great Falls. Maybe my friend Corey will go with me."

The next morning Corey and I headed for the highway in time to see the sun climb over a rim of buttes. After seeing nothing but plastered walls for nearly a year, it was a beautiful sight. By the side of the road each blade of new-born grass picked up the reflection, as if lit by individual lights.

People feel sorry for young hitchhikers in the desert, so right off, Corey and I got a ride. At the turnoff, we scrambled over the truck's tailgate and again stuck out our thumbs. By now the sun was a blazing globe, and the straight-arrow highway waved with heat, frying a rattler flattened by a passing tire.

A VW-bus whined toward us and stopped. The woman driver, wearing a long, psychedelic-colored dress, asked where we were going.

"If you boys need a place to stay, I know one. Free. Lots of grass."

Sounded good. Corey and I had only ten dollars between us.

"And you will learn to get in touch with your former selves."

I looked at Corey. She was in outer space, but we were broke. I half shuddered. She sounded like my counselor.

In Great Falls she pulled up to an old house and motioned us to go in.

"Welcome to our chateau, where one is always mountain high." The greeter sat at a table filling gelatin capsules with a purple powder. His shoulder-length pony-tailed hair bounced to his convulsive laughter.

Old mattresses and sleeping bags scattered around the living room's floor. With his bare foot, he kicked toward an empty spot. "Throw down your beds. Drop some acid. Name's Anton."

"I've never tried acid," I said. "What does it do?"

"Everything, Man. You hear colors. It's a rainbow road to another world."

The woman who brought us to the house glided past. "Anton will read the tarot cards tonight. Anton has the gift."

I decided to stay away from her. She was creepy. Like my counselor.

The rest of the house looked okay. The house was one of a number in Great Falls making up an informal commune. Drug traffickers for the local air force base flowed from one house to another. And for the next few weeks, so did Corey and I. I skyrocketed on the LSD. Thanks to Anton's advice, I could hear a fly walking on the window.

No one paid much attention to us, and we never needed money. When junkies are high, they're hospitable.

"Hey, Kid. I got some salami and cheese. Fill up."

So we made the rounds, stayed loaded and fairly well-fed, and learned a lot about drugs.

But one day, whoosh—a hunting knife whizzed past my head and stuck in the wall. I jumped out of my skin.

"Listen when I talk to ya, Kid! You got anything on you?"

"No," I stammered. "Nothing."

The guy walked over and pulled out his knife. His hands shook. He held the knife blade under Corey's nose. "I gotta have a fix. Now. I saw you with stuff last night. Don't hold out on me, or your throat is slit."

For some reason drugs hadn't been as plentiful as before.

"I don't have anything," pleaded Corey. "We'll see if we can get some."

At another house a guy loaded and unloaded his automatic. Anton was there. He pointed to us and in a strange voice intoned, "These two have not sacrificed before me. I demand it, now."

Corey and I split. Later, when I learned that Anton became the high priest of the satanistic church in a large city, and wrote the satanist bible, it didn't surprise me. What did surprise me—it was like a miracle—was that something prevented me from becoming part of that evil.

* * *

"I thought you were going to be gone all summer." I detected frustration in my mother's voice.

My stepfather slapped me. "Pot head. Don't come around here lookin' for free food."

I called him a couple of names and headed downtown where I flopped around the rest of the summer. In September, I tried school again, but the same old situations cropped up. After a few months I went back to the culture where I felt accepted. The satan worshipper and his friends had introduced me to the bottomless pit of shooting up and I bobsledded down it on a speed run.

The guys who paid the rent on the lice and bedbug infested apartments trafficked LSD and speed. We cut and packaged purple acid in gelatin caps. Powerful and profitable. We marketed speed or made hashish. Just kids but we knew our business and made a profit.

One day the door of an old house where I was staying, burst open.

38

"Police! We've got a Probable Cause warrant. Line up!"

Someone who thought they hadn't gotten their fair share of profits had squealed that we were shooting up. The cops searched our shoes, waistbands, everything, looking for evidence.

I was nervous. We had used up our speed, but the soaks and needles were thrown in the sink with a mountain of dirty dishes. They were in plain sight. But while the cops tore the place apart, they didn't see what they wanted. The cotton and powder blended with the dried spaghetti.

"Leavin' with your tails between your legs, officers?"

I thought my friend was out of his head, being so cocky.

"Look what we found growing out back," announced a plain-clothesman. "Pot."

"How far from the house?" The head narc's eyes glinted in satisfaction.

"'Bout a hundred feet."

The agent cursed. "It has to be under seventy-five feet from the house before we can attach it. And these punks knew it." He glowered at me. "Christensen, the other night I saw you pointing me out to a bunch of heavies. Thought you'd blow my cover. Well, we may not have anything today, but now I've got a fix on you. I'll know every move you make from now on."

My muscles relaxed and I shrugged. "Okay, Grady, if you want to spend your time, but I'm clean."

A tenth grader and already the police were on my tail. After that I made it my business to get over on them any time I could.

* * *

The probation officer caught up with me the next summer. "Monty, you're in trouble unless you go back to your family and to school."

I wouldn't go to my folks, but my grandmother lived in the trailer house next to theirs. I would ask her.

Grandmother poured coffee from an old aluminum coffee pot. "I can't take you in every time you get in trouble. Since your grandfather died, I can't afford the extra food or electricity."

She tilted the milk carton over her cup until the coffee was cinnamon colored, and sighed. "But you have to go to school. Make something of yourself. I pray that every day. All right, but mind, you get in early, nights. I won't be worryin' about you." She jabbed the stirring spoon into the coffee's depths and clanked the cup to emphasize her words.

That year I steady-dated a girl in school. My folks were happy.

"Marry her, Monty. She's crazy about you, and

marriage will settle you down."

She was a nice chick, but I hadn't thought of myself as being in love. I wasn't sure what that was. But my parents pushed and rail-roaded and signed the consent form because I wasn't eighteen, and the day she graduated, we headed to the justice of the peace.

We played house. I got a job driving a silage truck. Hot, sweaty, smelly work, and I hated it. I had cut down on hard drugs, but boozed it up most nights with pot thrown in when possible. The job lasted only a few weeks, and so did the job after that.

A wife, responsibility, bills, what people expected of me. I couldn't handle anything. I ran.

I ran back to the flop-house friends, failure written across my forehead. The knowledge that I let everyone down seared like a smoking branding iron, and my only aim in life was to dull the pain. I made drugs a full-time occupation and shot up in a frenzy with new acquaintances from California communes.

Sometimes I composed music and tried to fantasize another kind of life, one where I was in a nightclub playing my guitar and singing,

I'm just a lonely boy,
A lonely, poor boy,
So lonely I could die....

And I almost did. The emergency-room doctor shook his head as he pronounced, "You have serum hepatitis. Your liver is twice its normal size. If you do make it, you won't live past thirty."

Maybe a part of me wanted to die. Maybe some-one whispered that I wouldn't have to live up to anymore expectations. Dying was no big deal. Only peace and quiet. Maybe I listened.

With that sentence hanging over me, I ran from the hospital, back to the life I knew, subsisting on crackers and maybe a half-pint of milk a day, and speed. Or downers when I had to get some sleep.

I borrowed a car and merged into the freeway drug traffic. Grady knew it. His shadow fell across mine every place I went, and being on speed made me paranoid about where he was. So when I drove around with a hundred pounds of marijuana in the trunk, my heart lodged at the base of my throat until the pot was sold.

One day I dissolved a hundred tablets of speed in a jar of water, dropped a piece of cotton on top and drew up a c.c.-and-a-half. I injected. The rush threw me against the wall. I slid down, trembling. Sweat poured out of every pore, and a blast furnace in my body turned on high. I was frying alive.

I tore off my shirt and sat on the floor. This time I'm going to buy it, I thought. I'm going to die. In a numb daze, I thought about death. The black hole. That's what death would be. I closed my eyes and waited. Hours later I got to my feet. I hadn't died. I had a reprieve. I didn't wonder why or if there would be any more.

4

Hazel Eyes

It's ironic that an old jail in a little town like Grangeville would be used to make me remember my past, and face what my life was.

My first cobwebby thoughts sorted themselves. Had there been anything good in my life? Holly was one.

"Holly," I said aloud. "I have to call her."

I yelled for the guard. "Gotta make an important call!"

"Not this time of night, Buddy."

I hit the bars with my palm. Maybe Holly wouldn't talk to me anyway. Wouldn't blame her. I lay my head back on the dirty pillow, staring at the ceiling, remembering the night I met Holly.

Each day, for me, had been like the one before. Inject speed, go to the bar closest to my current residence, and drink beer. One night, head reeling, I was in the Jekyll and Hyde Bar, propped against a booth wall, listening to "Fifty Ways to Lose Your Lover."

"A girl wants to dance with you, Monty," said a friend. He pointed to a table where several girls sat.

I lurched over, pulled one of them onto the floor, and danced. Then I found my way back to the booth and sat down.

"Stupe," my friend hissed. "You danced with the wrong broad."

"Too bad," I said. "I'm not leaving again."

A few minutes later a slender creature with long brown hair slid onto the seat across from me.

"Hi," she said. "I'm Holly, and I'm reading a book that says if you're interested in someone, you're supposed to tell them. So I just wanted to tell you that I'm interested in you." She laughed and waited.

I looked at her through a salmon-colored haze. She was no bar floozy. What was going on? Didn't she know I was out of it? I'd never had a come-on like this before, but she was a looker. Dressed nice. Maybe she had a few dollars to loan me. My present financial situation wasn't good.

"They're closing," I said. "Why don't you come over to my old lady's house?"

"Your mom's?" She sounded surprised.

"No, my ex-wife's. I'm staying with her for a few days."

44

Holly's blue eyes—or maybe hazel—widened.

"No big deal," I said. "Didn't have any other place to go."

We sat outside the house in Holly's yellow Mustang and talked. She was running from her home life, too.

"Mom has always been too busy with her career to pay attention to me," she said. "Dad did, but he died a couple of years ago. I don't feel as if I belong anywhere."

We talked until the sun lighted up Indian Ridge. She left and I went in to sprawl on the couch.

When I awakened, the dream of blue-gray eyes vanished with the sickening feeling that I needed a fix.

* * *

A few days later I was on her doorstep. "As long as we're both running, want to do it together? We can go to Seattle and hang around."

I expected her to refuse. Why would a classy girl want to hang out with me?

"Sure," she said. "Sounds like fun."

We spent a couple of days there, then headed back to Great Falls and set up house. The rent ate up most of our money, so we lived on pancakes. Pancakes and cocaine. Holly was acquainted with marijuana, but I expanded her horizons. The first time I stuck the needle in her arm, she looked the other way. After awhile it became a morning ritual to get high together.

I also introduced her to the drug's financial district. Charley was my middleman, delivering my coke and bringing me back the money while he skimmed his own profit off the top. He knew a lot of people, all over the country.

One night he came over. "I've got a proposition for you," he said. "Some people in Boston told me to ask you to go back and sign a pact."

"What do you mean, a pact?"

"You work for them, and they give you power. Like you could light a three-dimensional fire in the corner of this living room. Just like that. Power, Man. You'd live in the country and keep away from people. That's all I know."

Holly looked at me in fright. "Monty, that's spooky."

I agreed. Besides, who knew me and would ask for me? Who did I know in those kinds of things? Visions of black pits and candles and Anton's tarot cards flooded my mind. Then there were the guys who had been involved in that world and had died. I could almost see bony fingers reaching for me. No thanks.

Holly was continually frightened by our life-style, as in the time Charley took my money and my coke, and skipped. I grabbed a gun, went to all the places where he usually crashed, and kicked down the doors.

"Where's Charley?" I yelled, waving the gun around. "Man, I'm goin' to blow off your kneecaps if you don't tell me where that no-good snake is!"

"Charley left the state, Monty. Don't know where he is, honest!"

After a few days my anger cooled, but Holly knew if I had gotten my hands on him I would have killed Charley, and she wondered aloud what she was into.

We sold Holly's Mustang for coke and had an old Rambler station wagon. She worked in a jewelry store, but we were broke and moved into a Smelterville motel. I got a graveyard shift at the smelter. I didn't like the work or the hours and quit after one week. But not before I again saw those beckoning fingers.

One of the guys in the mine was at our place one night. "I'm a satanist," he said. "I've got power. If I wanted to kill one of the guys at the job, I'd just have to think it. Presto."

"Sure," I laughed, although somehow I believed it.

He stared at me a few seconds and said, "If you were on the highway and were hit by a car, you would leave your body for a moment and be suspended over it. Then you'd come back to your body with more power than you can imagine."

Our gaze locked. He was repulsive. Why hadn't I noticed that before?

Suddenly I found myself walking across the interstate. Cars whooshed and honked around me. Somehow I got to the shoulder and hitched a ride home. The guy was gone.

I've told myself that I relived an LSD trip or that I was high and didn't know where I was going. But however you figure it, I should have been killed. Just like the guy said "presto."

Why did I meet these kinds of people? One after another were sent my way. Weird ones. Satanists. Like I was a prize catch. But why *hadn't* I been killed on the highway? Maybe I was a prize—for two different sides.

* * *

The past gave way to the present as the Grangeville police shoved a drunk in the cell next to mine. A putrid cloud accompanied him. I lay on the unforgiving steel bunk. Plenty of times I smelled like that. A great life. Ha. Why had I messed up everything? Especially with Holly?

"Oh, Holly." I squeezed shut my eyes. "Your whole life spiraled downhill when you met me. Straight down."

After the mining company, we went back to Billings, and with no money, lived in the station wagon. Holly was pregnant, and her mother put the screws on me to marry her daughter. Part of me wanted to— to be a dad and settle down and all that, but I couldn't stand the pressure. I said I didn't have to do anything, and I ran. Moved in with a buddy from work.

Holly's brother called. "Christensen, Holly is in Oregon having an abortion."

"What's an abortion?" That was a new term to me.

"Jerk, she's getting rid of the baby. You ought to pay for it."

I didn't listen to much else he said. I didn't know it was possible to get rid of a baby. My baby. I thought about that. I had no feeling about it one way or the other. While I cared about Holly, I realized deep down that I used her. I knew she loved me, and that made me feel good. Whatever made me feel good was what I wanted.

Holly called when she got home and cried because the ordeal had been so bad. I reacted by being angry at her and her mother for not telling me about the abortion, and her brother for hounding me for money.

I didn't know what real love was. I couldn't feel her pain.

It was a couple of weeks before I saw her again; the next time I needed her.

* * *

Grady and another narcotic agent, McAllister, continued to heel my steps like trained pigs. One night in the Jekyll and Hyde, my friends and I had downed a few beers when the agents came in, trying to pass as part of the crowd.

"Hey, look," I said to a new guy in town. "Those two are narcs. Watch out."

"Oh, yeah?" His bleary eyes focused on the figures. "Hate narcs. I'll fix 'em." He threw his full beer bottle across the room. It hit one of the cops in the forehead and broke, cutting him bad.

The next night my friends and I closed up the bar. As we left, two black-and-whites screeched to a stop in front of the place. Before I knew what was happening, a bunch of cops grabbed me. Fists smashed into my nose and eyes, my stomach, my groin. I sank to the ground and was thrown in one of the cars. At the jail, they dragged me out and smashed my face into an iron grate. Inside, they hit me again. My face was numb. Blood poured from my nose and from under my eye, rivuleted down my neck and dropped on the floor.

"What...charges?" I mumbled, not able to lift my head.

"We've got enough to make up for the hassle you've given us, Christensen. For starters, assaulting an officer. You've got a court date in the morning."

They pushed me to a stairwell and gave me a shove. I couldn't stop the fall.

"Did you trip and hurt yourself? Be more careful."
The cops were enjoying themselves.

I couldn't answer. Every bone in my body seemed
bent out of shape. Let me in that court tomorrow, I
thought. I'll tell the judge what happened. I'll tell
everybody!

The next morning I was awake. Puffy, covered
with crusty blood, hurting ribs, but ready to go to
court. I waited. An hour later, I yelled for the guard.

"What time am I supposed to be in court?"

"Oh, my," said the guard, slapping his cheek like
Jack Benny. "It was an hour ago. We told the judge
we couldn't wake you. Quite a hangover you had,
Christensen. Tsk, tsk."

"You dirty..." I shook the bars. "You pigs didn't
want the judge to see me. Afraid he'd know what
happened!"

I seethed with hate and rage. "I need to make a
phone call!"

"Holly! I need help. You've got to get me out of
here!"

An hour later, with Holly's signature on a bond,
and knowing there would be a warrant for my arrest,
we loaded the Rambler and skipped town.

* * *

We ran for Yellowstone Park and joined summer vacation collegiates in laundry and snack-bar jobs. While Holly worked, the drug suppliers, intertwining among the squeaky cleans, kept me in pot. The campground or mid-lake boating parties were higher than Old Faithful.

One person who didn't join in was a girl who read her Bible during lunch breaks. She got teased, especially by me. I enjoyed getting people to laugh at her. I didn't see anything wrong with it. She set herself up by being "religious."

For several weeks, life was a party, complete with trick playing. One worker had his tires suspended from the top of a lodgepole pine. I felt sorry for him and climbed up and cut them down. But a national park was no sanctuary against the power that stalked me.

The night I tried to help someone was the night that power tried to close in on me.

A kid who worked in the park was deep into heavy acid. My talking at him about it didn't help. One night while Holly was working, he came to our cabin, really messed up, his face swollen and green. After weeks of partying, I was trying to cut down on drugs and hadn't had any for awhile. But I scrambled for something to get him down from his high. I talked to him, trying to keep him in reality.

As I talked, he changed. Looking at me were not the eyes of a messed-up boy, but others—evil ones. My skin felt like spiders were crawling on it. I had seen those eyes before, in those who belonged to

Satan.

The kid left. As I stared after him, the back of my neck pricked. A presence, so strong I could almost touch it, spread through the room. The wall bowed. From deep within, I knew what was happening. Satan had come for me. I screamed and heard myself screaming a name I didn't know was real.

"God, help me! God, help me!"

As I shrieked that name, the pressure lessened, but when I stopped, the force, the intensity, was again in the room and on me. The walls bowed again. I ran into the night and almost blew down the door to the religious girl's cabin. Somehow, she could help me.

"Satan's trying to get me! Help me, please help me!"

"Sit down, Monty. It'll be okay."

She pulled on her bathrobe and opened her Bible to the first chapter of John. "In the beginning...."

She read and read. I hadn't heard any of this before, but wasn't really listening to the words. I just knew Satan couldn't get me now. She kept reading and then prayed for me. Everything subsided and I was at peace.

I thanked her and stepped out into the tangy pine, and damp earth air. I breathed in, letting the pungence wash through me. Crystal stars fitted against the sky in an order I never before noticed. There was an order to everything. The world wasn't made to be just any which way. Maybe personal lives weren't either. Instead of "anything goes," maybe lives were meant to be in right order with something.

The pine-needled path muffled my steps as I walked and thought. It was as though a door had swung open a crack, enough to see light on the other side.

Holly waited for me. The cabin was peaceful.

"We're getting out of here," I said, the second I crossed the threshhold.

I told her what happened. "Sweetheart, I've thought about us. We shouldn't be living together. That's wrong."

She didn't understand, and argued with me the rest of the night, but the next morning we drove to Phoenix. Even with the previous night's happening, I was still scared and running.

We rented an apartment, but I was restless, my stomach in knots. We owed money to the bondsman, and now I knew, whatever the consequences, it had to be paid.

We drove back through Nevada. At midnight crossing Hoover Dam, I got goose bumps. An electric feeling. Not hair-standing-up-on-the-back-of-the-neck kind, but elating, happy. Not having any religious background, I didn't realize that it was God's touch. I only knew something needed changing. I wasn't living the right life. I steered with one hand and clasped Holly's hand with the other.

"Holly, the way we're living is wrong. Please

marry me. If you don't, our relationship is through. I'm sorry, but I won't live like this anymore."

Holly pulled away her hand. "You're not giving me any choice, are you? All right. If you want to."

Her lack of enthusiasm surprised me, but I was determined to make things right—for both of us.

An hour later, in T-shirts and jeans, we awakened a Las Vegas justice of the peace, bought a fifteen-dollar ring, a thirty-dollar wedding, and a pint of whiskey for celebrating.

5

Bitter 'n' Sweet

I tried. We lived in a basement apartment in Billings, and I got a job packing concrete forms for Montana's eight-foot basements. A skinny kid crawling in and out of holes, packing forms ten and twelve hours a day. Pouring calcium-laced concrete in fifteen-degrees-below-zero.

I made it without drugs and heavy drinking for a couple of months. Then my willpower ran out. I was tired of trying to be good and do good. On payday I was back at the drug and bar scene. Sometimes I didn't make it home.

I had been tapped on the shoulder about certain areas of my life, but I wasn't sure by whom. I had yelled to God for help, but who knew what God was? Some kind of power. All I had was my own.

Holly was pregnant again, and we needed money. Drug dealing was the fastest way to get it.

I was now considered by many to be an area heavy. The one with answers. A couple of cons from Colorado taught me how to rip off drug dealers. Risky business—they kill for revenge, but I got good and could pull ten thousand dollars out of a person's pocket without their realizing it. I also got good at disappearing when the pigeons learned who plucked them. After all, this was home territory.

I was doing what I liked best. Getting it over on people and getting loaded.

Meanwhile, my boss kept at me about going to church. I didn't want any of that, but figured he had money and I needed it. If I did what he wanted, maybe we could switch.

The night Holly and I went with him, we were corralled at the altar. Holly cried, I wasn't sure why, and I acted as if it were a great uplifting experience, but I don't think my boss and his wife were fooled.

They sicked their minister on us. He and his wife often dropped by to visit. They figured we were a nice couple who should go to church. Holly enjoyed it, but I'd sit there wishing I could get my stash out of the desk drawer and get high.

One evening while trying to buy a kilo, I barely made it out with my skin intact. I drove home and exploded through the front door with, "I got shot at!"

The minister and his wife sat in the living room. Holly was mad at me for days.

The life I wanted to live motivated me to plug into heavier dealers. To organized crime. If I got close to the Mexican border, I could make connections with a shipper, take the drugs to Montana, and be one of the kingpin dealers. That was as appealing as the money.

Holly and I were fighting, so I didn't bother to tell her. I just took off for New Mexico.

A roommate, found through the classifieds, got me involved with a forgery-and-armed-robbery ring. I was arrested for burglary. While in jail I heard that Oregon slackened its marijuana laws. The first state to make three ounces or less only a misdemeanor. The day I got out, I stuffed my twenty-five automatic in my pocket and headed my car north.

* * *

Conscience sprinkled a topping on my need for money, and I called Holly from Portland.

"Hi, Babe. Are we parents yet?"

There was a long pause, then her soft voice edged with tears. "Three weeks ago. Where have you been?"

"I've had business to take care of. What did we have? Boy or girl?"

"We had a blue-eyed boy. I named him Jared, the way we planned."

She wasn't talkative. I tried to lighten things. "Blue eyes. Doesn't sound like *my* son! Ha, ha. Well, that's great. I'll be seeing you real soon, but I need money to get home. Been staying here with friends.

Wire me some money, will you?"

"Money!" The flash fire from her voice burned through the wires and seared my ear. "Monty, when you disappeared, I moved in with Mom and I'm on welfare. Ninety dollars a month. You left me with a baby and nothing...nothing but your bills. Stay out of my life!"

I winced as I hung up. She sounded mad.

A few days later, when friends wouldn't loan me any more money for beer and pot, I tried Holly again.

"Honey, I want to get back to see you and my son. Maybe you could ask your mom for money."

"After what you've done? Mom wouldn't loan you a tumbleweed!" Her voice softened. "But Mom's brother-in-law, my Uncle Truman, lives in Corvallis, not far from Portland. Maybe if you went there, he'd loan you enough to come back."

"I'm on my way." Suddenly my future looked brighter. A fresh patsy.

My friends bought me enough gas for a one-way trip, and I headed down the freeway, planning my con job or burglary or whatever. I'd play it by ear.

* * *

I parked across the street from the small white house and surveyed things. The yard was tidy.

Flowers and a birdhouse. A picture of square people. Easy pickings, but I'd better leave the motor running. Uncle Truman knew about the abortion. Maybe he'd come at me with a shotgun.

When he answered the door I began the con. "Hello, Truman. Holly told me if I were ever in this area to stop and say hello. And I just happened to be passing through."

To my surprise, the little guy answered, "Monty, I'm happy to meet you. I've heard so much about you." He peered past me. "You left your motor running. Park your car by the garage."

Wow. This man was naive. Maybe he didn't have both oars in the water, or all of his muffins weren't done, or something. But that was okay.

He and his wife Mildred bumped into each other getting dinner for me. Truman set the table with his left hand. His right arm hung stiffly at his side. "Monty, please stay overnight," he pleaded.

"Well...." I hesitated the right amount of time. "Okay."

I was enjoying myself. After dinner I went to the medicine cabinet to see what drugs they had. I checked the bedroom to see how much money was there. I would wait for the right time and take Uncle Truman for what I could. A loan or anything. Maybe after he was asleep I would make off with something. I wouldn't stick around.

"Uncle Truman, I'm going to walk around Corvallis."

He smiled and nodded as if that were what he had hoped I'd do.

I went to a bar, smoked pot, had a few beers, went back to the house, and passed out.

The next morning Mildred fixed ham and eggs and biscuits. While I ate, I told them all the good things I'd done, all the good things I was going to do, all the potential I had, how wonderful I was. They listened as though it was worth listening to.

Later we sat on their lawn swing. I was playing Truman like a fish I intended to land, when he said, "Monty, if I had a son, I'd want him to be like you. I love you."

Tears gathered in his eyes. I had to get out of there, so I took off for the tavern to smoke pot and drink. It was strange. I couldn't get drunk. I couldn't get happy. Nothing worked. All I could hear was Truman saying, "I love you, Monty...a son just like you."

It was plain that he knew all about me, but he cared about me. I was important. I wasn't able to verbalize those feelings then; it was all muddy water in my mind.

The next morning I made the decision not to take anything from Uncle Truman, not even borrow money. He treated me like a son and loved me like one. He was the only friend I'd ever had, so I would let it stay that way—that I had one friend in my life and hadn't done him wrong. That was one of the only moral things I had ever done.

There was an atmosphere about the house that I couldn't pinpoint. Maybe the paint on the walls had a special tint. Maybe they were religious people, but both Holly and I had run into religious people before, and they shook their fists in our faces and told us we were going to hell and would burn there for eternity. But there was something different here, so I wouldn't take anything from him.

It took all day to get the courage to tell Truman. I sat him on the hassock and sat next to him. I said, "Listen, Truman, I lied to you. I came to steal from you. I'm not what I told you. I've been in mental institutions, the state hospital, the reform school, in and out of jail, and foster homes. I left your niece with a child. All I do is drugs and alcohol. I'm sorry I came, and don't worry, I'm leaving."

He teared up and that was a lousy time to leave, so I sat there not knowing what to do.

He shook his head. "Son, I love you. It doesn't make any difference what you've done or where you've been or what's happened in your life. I love you and you're special to me."

I felt as though something warm was pouring through me.

He said, "Monty, you were created for life. Not for death. When God made you He created you in His own image. He wanted to walk beside you. To talk with you. To fellowship with you. For you to be His friend." Truman brushed the back of his hand across his face and looked me in the eye. "God gives life, but the things you are doing are working death for you.

Son, that's why you have problems and pain. It's all that destruction going on in your life."

I uneasily shifted position on the hassock. I'd never heard anything like this before. He was an old man. Maybe he believed in fairy tales.

"See, Monty. God's first creations, the ones He made for His pleasure, violated His first law and fell under the curse of sin and death. Just as He had warned them. They fell under Satan's power. You were born under this bondage."

Satan's power. I looked at Truman in amazement. Did he know about my encounters with that power? The counselor's seances? Anton? The satanist who wanted to kill me, and the tremendous evil force in the Yellowstone cabin? There were other times that dark power showed itself. I knew it was true, so what Truman said made sense.

"You mean," I said, "that Satan is out to get us. I've experienced that."

"Right," said Truman. "We're born under that curse, and he does everything he can to keep us. What he does is try to get our lives to be controlled by everything but God."

"What do you mean?"

"Monty, your life has been controlled by your flesh. That means whatever you wanted to do controlled what you did. You were controlled by drugs and alcohol and an immoral life-style. But Monty, that's not why you were created and that's why things are out of kilter for you."

The things he said were like a hot fireplace poker searing my insides. I was tempted to run and yet something deep inside compelled me to listen.

"Monty, in John 3:16 of God's Word, He says He loves you so much that He sent His son Jesus to die in your place on Calvary. For all the things you've done. You deserve to die because of your sins. But Son, He forgives seventy times seven and even beyond."

Seventy times seven? I sucked in my breath as I remembered writing in the dust, and my friend who fixed my bike. In a flash the filth, the stench and blackness of my life were before me. It didn't matter what state I was in. Whether Montana or New Mexico or Idaho—no difference. The filth and stench were there. I couldn't get away from it. Not in any kind of drug or alcohol or relationship. That's what I had wanted to do—get away from the hurts given to me and the hurts I'd given to others.

In the unconditional love in Uncle Truman, I saw the presence of an unconditional, loving God. To someone like me—and man, I knew how filthy I was.

"Monty, if you ask Jesus to forgive you and come into your life, He'll do it and will break those chains. He'll bring you to the purpose for which you were created."

So on June 6, 1974, I got down on my knees with little Truman Dragoo. The words were hesitant, but I meant them more than anything I had ever said in my life.

"Jesus, I believe that You died for me. That even if I had been the only person on earth, You would have done that for me. Forgive me of my sin. I believe Your Word that You forgive anyone who asks. Come into my life and be Lord of it. I can't do anything right on my own, so I give myself to You. I've asked and now I believe You have saved me from an eternal death, and have made me a new man."

Wow. Suddenly it was like a symphony of crystal bells went off inside me. The jolt from every upper I had ever had was nothing compared to the high I had at that moment. My life had been eruptive and emotional, and so was my turn-around. I laughed and cried. Uncle Truman said later he'd never seen anything like it. A triumphal entry through heaven's gates for one Satan thought he had in his hip pocket.

* * *

Right away I started reading the Bible. I couldn't read it enough. I couldn't imagine that this Jesus, about whom I had never heard, had done all the things I was reading about.

Everything became alive. I had never noticed colors before I accepted Christ. Dazzling blues and greens. The flowers in Truman's yard invited me to inhale their fragrance.

I had always thought that down the road I would find my pot of gold. I thought I was lucky and would get that break. I never did.

Until I met Jesus face to face, I had no idea what my life was all about. But now I knew. I was alive and knew why. The minute I allowed Christ into my life, I understood. Things made sense.

"I have to call Holly," I said to a geranium. "No, I haven't talked to her since I've been here. She won't believe me. I'll get a job first."

I didn't know that Mildred called Holly each time I was out of the house. Holly was hearing strange things.

I got a job in an auto parts store. Armed with my happiness with the Jesus who had set me free and my Bible, which was unfolding great and wonderful things, I preached to everyone.

A friend said later, "When Monty got saved, God gave him a great ministry—to teach patience to older Christians."

But I had come from the bottom of a dark well into sunshine and had to tell everyone.

A few days after getting the job, I called Holly. "Listen, Dear, things are really different. I'm different. I don't drink or do drugs or the other stuff I did. I met Jesus. He's set me free. I love you and wish you were here."

"Do you know how many calls I've had before about how you had changed and were going to do good?" Holly's voice shook with anger. "Now you're going religious. Well, I know you and there's nothing...nothing that could change you, so lay off trying to con me!"

In my high hopes, I hadn't thought about that response. Silently I handed the phone to Uncle Truman and went to the front window to stare at a blurry street.

Words from Truman's conversation floated across me. "...and I allow You to come into my life and be Master...."

I whirled. Truman was leading Holly in the sinner's prayer. She was accepting! I yelled for joy. God did it. He did it!

I picked up Holly at the airport. She was beautiful. I loved her so much. She handed me a compact, warm bundle. I looked down at the face of my son and couldn't keep the tears away.

"Two babies were birthed in this family," I said softly.

Holly understood what I mean. "Huh-uh. Don't forget me....There were three," she laughed.

* * *

That was a sweet time. We lived a couple of miles from town in a trailer house that had a couch, chair, and bed. But we picked blackberries that grew in towering thickets, and when we doused the shining berries with sugar and milk, we didn't notice our thorn-ripped skin. Or we would go canoeing or fishing. Sometimes Mildred watched Jared while Holly and I drove to the ocean.

Uncle Truman was ecstatic. One day he said, "You know, many years ago God called me to minister to people with music. My piano was my life until this stroke." He touched his rigid right arm. "My ministry was over. I was of no more use to God and I couldn't understand why He kept me here. Now I do. He had a different, but wonderful job for me—leading you and Holly to Him. I feel so privileged."

For a few months, we attended Truman's Bible-believing church, but while the sermons were good salvation ones, they didn't satisfy the thirst I had to learn more about God and what He had for me, so Holly and I tried another church. We sat in the service only a few minutes before I knew this was home.

We attended a Friday night believer's fellowship with praising and singing. I preached to everyone I met, on and off the job. Lots of people avoided me, even Christians, because I was a fanatic, but that was their problem. I felt I was called to do exactly what I was doing—make money and preach. This was the culmination of my walk with the Lord.

However, one day, an experience shook me. As I walked down the gravel road to the mailbox, a three dimensional motion picture suddenly flashed before me. Every detail of the picture was imprinted on my mind. A three-story brick facility. Trafficking through the doors were what I instinctively knew were social lepers—people society shunned.

The mental camera zoomed in on an office window. As I looked into the room, a strange feeling swept over me. I knew each piece of furniture. I knew whose office it was. It was mine!

At the mailbox the vision ended. I felt like Ebeneezer Scrooge in Dicken's *Christmas Carol*. So much happened in such a brief time. But what did it mean? The enormity of it put me on my face before the Lord.

"Lord, tell me."

Most of the time God doesn't speak from a burning bush or neon the answer from a tall building. Most of the time He gently opens a door, and if we're listening to His voice, we'll go through it.

Not long after that, Christian musicians approached me. "Monty, we're going to the prison in Salem. With your background in reform school and the drug-and-alcohol scene, why don't you come with us and speak to the men?"

I didn't hesitate a moment. "No," I said, "those guys had their chance. They've all had a chance and have rejected God. If they hadn't they wouldn't be in prison. I'm not going in there."

6

Downhill Spiral

Was my self-righteous, deliberate refusal to step through the open door the thing that caused my spiral downhill? I doubt it. God forgives. He would have given me another chance, and the two of us would have started over again.

However, I went from one extreme to the other. From hell to heaven with no stopping on planet earth.

While I led people to Christ, I still had the life-style imprint of before. Old habits were still with me. Not just smoking and occasional drinking, but the pattern of getting angry with job conditions or my boss and either quitting or being fired.

Or there was the old financial problem. Going into debt. We owed for the couch, the chair, another car, and were in debt to Truman for the use of his gas cards.

I hadn't dealt with my old weaknesses and life patterns, and they all reared their heads at one time. Communication with Holly was back to zip. We weren't on the same wavelength. Smoldering resentments burst into flame.

"Monty, why did you leave the job at the grocery store? Look at the bills." Holly flipped through the stack on the table.

"Honey, you know the manager had it in for me because I'm a Christian. He got sarcastic when I witnessed to customers. I couldn't take that. The Lord will provide for us."

"Baloney! You're just doing what you've always done—jumping from one job to another. You won't settle down although you've got a family to support. You've always left me stuck with bills, and I suppose you'll do it again."

"Yeah, well, you want everything under the sun, the way your mom gave you."

That scene repeated itself. Each time I lost a job, I saw more frowns from people I cared about. Rejection. Pressure from every direction was overwhelming, and I reverted to my old pattern of running from stress. I got loaded on pot, and then the guilt piled on, and I ran from that. I had never learned to handle responsibility and stress. The bobsled was on its way down, and I didn't know how to stop it.

I couldn't tell anyone at church. They all had smiles that said everything was perfect in their lives. No one ever said he had problems. They'd pray that the Lord would give them jobs or bring back wayward children. Their sharing never had anything to do with *them*. They told how close they were to the Lord and how He had all their external circumstances under control. So I figured that once a person accepts Christ, he doesn't have anymore struggles or temptations. If I told them about the turmoil and gunk inside me, they'd think I wasn't a Christian. I must not be one. What was the use of trying?

What had happened to me was real. Jesus Christ was real, but I couldn't handle the Christian walk.

Holly and I started drinking again. I heard wine was supposed to be okay, but I couldn't drink just one glass. I would finish the bottle.

Since I was uncomfortable around church people, I searched out the other kind, the kind from my old life-style and smoked a few joints with them. After that, I brought home a bag of pot.

Before I knew it, my conscience callous was hardening. I smoked pot before Sunday evening church and went to the services loaded to the gills.

Holly and I were moving farther away from the Lord. Everybody saw it. The looks we got in church told us that. Our Christian neighbors admonished us about our life-style, and I told them where they could go.

* * *

It was finished. Our walk with the Lord, the sweet times. It was over. We put all our still-owed-for furniture in storage and hit the Montana trail.

In Billings I got a job and tried to pull myself up, but Holly and I would fight or something would happen to discourage me, and I'd give up.

I was bound with the same chains as before, but now they were stronger, tighter. I got back into heavy cocaine, and stayed away from home, and usually passed out at someone's house after partying all night.

So I wasn't surprised when the messenger at the door handed me divorce papers. Holly had had enough.

Oh, well, I thought. That's the way my life goes.

I headed for Missoula and checked out the scene with a friend who was released on a burglary sentence and was into B'hai. After I listened to him, I said, "This is a bunch of garbage. You're nuts!"

Even in my degenerated state I knew the cult wasn't the truth that I had once had. Besides, vegetarianism didn't fit into my life-style.

My style dictated the good things, I thought. Holly was part of that. I still loved her and missed little Jared. I wanted to show her I had done well. That I was Somebody. In fantasy, I saw myself driving up to her in a fancy car. But how to get it? The only person I knew who might give me money was Grandma.

But Grandma wasn't an easy touch. When I arrived at her doorstep, she was glad to see me, but up front made sure I knew she wouldn't give me money. There went my plan to impress Holly and the drug dealers.

I was angry. Just a few thousand stood between me and the good life. Old memory tapes from childhood played through my mind. "Get it over on people if you have to."

I forged Grandma's name on a five-thousand-dollar check and made tracks for a car dealer.

After driving away, I stopped at a phone booth. "Holly, it's Monty. Let's get back together. Grandma gave me my share of her estate so we can make a new life." In my cocaine-fuzzed mind, that wasn't a lie. "I've got a Cadillac Eldorado. You'll like it, and we'll get our furniture out of storage and begin again."

Holly gave an excited laugh. "That sounds good."

"Great," I said. "but first I have to make a deal in Wyoming. Be back soon."

The "deal" included partying, and I stayed longer than I intended.

"Christensen," someone said, "the word's around there's a forgery rap out for you."

I ran for the nearest phone. "Grandma, I'm sorry about the check. Forgive me. Please don't press charges, and I'll come home and pay you back."

"I'm sorry, Monty, but I can't undo it. It isn't in my hands anymore."

"Oh, great!" I yelled, banging the receiver. "My

own grandmother!"

I was on the run. I went to Missoula and my B'hai friend and I stashed the car until I could switch plates. I was scared, and I got loaded so I didn't have to face the trouble I was in.

Would anyone help me? Uncle Truman. He'd do something. I had to get down to Portland.

I took off through the back roads and over the old mountain pass. Grangeville was the next town.

* * *

Good old Grangeville. I sat in it's Alamo-type jail, waiting until they found the evidence—the cocaine I had thrown out the car window. They would charge me with stealing the Plymouth and resisting arrest. Then they'd add everything against me. This was the end.

I slammed my hand down on the bed. All the remembering was to try to figure out how I got in this mess. What had gone wrong? What had happened to the "good life"?

It was too late to go back and begin again. I had used up God's forgiveness of seventy times seven. It was too late, wasn't it?

I leaped to my feet and shook the door. "Guard! I want to talk to a pastor!"

❖ ❖ ❖

7

Holly

1976

"T.G.I.F., Holly. Time to quit. Let's have a belt."

Holly pulled the cover over the typewriter and smiled at her boss. He reminded her of Daddy, especially after a couple of drinks. Jovial and fun-loving.

The office staff gathered around the reception desk and as plastic glasses refilled, laughter became louder and remarks more suggestive.

An hour later, backing out of the parking lot, Holly giggled. "Like Daddy used to say, 'I'm not mad at anybody.' Right now, not even ex-husband Monty—wherever he is."

In the mobile home she shared with her mother, a pan of spaghetti sauce bubbled on the stove, its sharp oregano aroma seeping under the lid. Jared sat in his high chair, with a "TODAY I AM A LITTLE DEER" bib around his neck.

Holly kissed his smooth cheek. "Hi, Sweety."

She turned to her mother. "Mom, thanks for getting him from daycare. The spaghetti smells good, but I'm not hungry. I had a lot of peanuts at the office." She talked faster at the admonishing look on her mother's face. "Think I'll shower and change and meet the gals for a movie. Would you mind watching Jared tonight? I won't be late."

"It's always two and three in the morning when you get in, Holly, but I love being with Jared."

"You sure have changed, Mom," Holly laughed. "I remember when you would throw a fit if I were out late."

Mrs. Moser cut a bowlful of spaghetti into manageable bites for Jared and poured a cup of milk.

"That was when you were with Monty. I knew the neighbors knew when you got in and when you didn't. But if you meet new friends and forget about him now, it's worth it." She set the cup down so hard milk sloshed. "Why you *ever* got mixed up with that loser, I'll never know. I just wish you had come to your senses earlier."

Anger rose inside Holly and the leftover office party glow couldn't stop the automatic torrent. "Well, at least when he was around, *he* paid attention to me. You were always too busy with your career or your bowling or your stupid bridge games. I came last on your priority list. So there's not a whole lot of difference, is there?"

Holly whirled and strode down the hallway. She shouldn't have said those things. She felt the same way about Monty that her mother did. But when Mom criticized him, she had to defend him.

The old animosity reared its head. Resentment against her tall, graceful mother that went back to elementary days.

Too many times her mother had said, "Don't hug me, Holly; you'll mess up my hair," or "Holly, I can't listen to your report, I'm late for bowling. Ask your father."

And later, "You've got a problem about *what*? Holly, I don't have time. If you have problems ask the good sisters at your school. That's why they're there."

In junior high when Holly made friends with a sophisticated "party girl" who introduced her to drinking, she would have welcomed even a spanking from her mother—any indication that she cared what happened to Holly.

But there was only impatient yelling. "That was stupid, Holly," or "Won't you ever learn?"

No, thought Holly, you were indifferent to me, Mom. The only time I touched you was when I made you mad.

She laughed. "And I sure did that plenty of times. Still do."

By the time Holly cinched the belt on the black-and-white jumpsuit and smoothed the fabric's sleekness, her mood had lightened. The outfit was a smart one that helped cover hurts although it took a big chunk out of her last paycheck. The only reason she could have bought it or the other clothes she splurged on since Monty left, was because Mom paid the major bills.

True, Mom had never been there. She always worked long hours and when she got home, ironed until midnight. Daddy's job kept him away from home a lot. He was affectionate to Holly, but Mother demonstrated her brand of love in Saturday shopping sprees.

Then Daddy died, and suddenly Mom suffocated Holly with possessiveness. "You're going out again tonight? Stay home with me. I'm lonely."

Holly stroked on mascara, then stood back and gazed into the mirror, seeing silhouettes of the recent past.

When she and Monty first lived together in Great Falls, when all they had to eat were pancakes, Mom had St. Vincent dePaul stop by with groceries. After Smelterville, when Holly was pregnant, Mom got them an apartment and furnished it with her own furniture. Mom was always there with whatever they needed, even though she didn't like the way they lived, or when it got down to it, Monty.

"A big part of that was pride," Holly said to the mirror.

Appearances were important. The Moser family had an image to uphold in their community and their church. Woe to anyone who threatened that image.

And that included a daughter and a granddaughter.

"Holly, you can't have this baby," her mother ordered, when Holly was pregnant for the first time. "I gave Monty a chance to make a respectable woman out of you, but he ran out, and you can't raise that child by yourself. You're young, you have no money. And if you don't think about that, think about me. The whole town will talk. I won't be able to hold up my head. My daughter—an unmarried mother. And what will Father Roarke say?" Her mother shook her brown coiffed head. "Holly, you must have an abortion. Then we can put this all behind us and begin again."

Holly was too confused to protest. Monty rejected her, Mom rejected the way she was. What else could she do but follow? So four months pregnant, she and her mother traveled to Oregon because it was one of the few states condoning abortions.

Holly clamped her hands over her head. "No, I won't remember that. I won't think about it!"

The trouble was, the memories lurked, waiting to ambush her when she least expected it. When she was alone for any length of time, scenes paraded across her mind like a slide-show.

The scenes were so real they made her sick. The hospital's green walls, the long needle injected in her abdomen, the waiting, the pain, the vomiting, the aloneness. Mom didn't stay. She went someplace—shopping or to meet friends.

And then the baby, there in the provided bedpan.

A baby girl, shriveled and burned red from saline.

"She would have been tall," Holly had whispered to the nurse who took the bedpan somewhere to dump.

* * *

The abortion scenes faded away, but Holly knew they would return. For now a movie would blanket the torturous memories, and later she and her friends would stop at Jekyll's for a few drinks and some laughs. She would have no time to wonder why Monty left, or where he was, or who he was with. Tomorrow she would repeat the pattern.

On the highway, she shifted the 'sixty-seven Mustang, a gift from Mom. Although it was a subtle reward for divorcing Monty, Mom always made sure Holly had a car.

Holly smiled, thinking of her first car. Mom picked it out in a car lot and Daddy paid seventy-five dollars for it. A red Ford with white interior that smelled like feet. Someone in bare feet had driven it across country during a hot summer. They never could get the odor out, but Holly hadn't cared. She named it "Arnold." When she was grounded for staying out late, Daddy took out the sparkplug wires. But she learned how to hook them back up, so that punishment hadn't worked.

Then came the yellow Mustang and now this one.

The others were sold to pay for drugs.

Stop it, Holly. No remembering allowed.

* * *

The movie wasn't as funny as the ads had said. One of the guys in it looked like Monty. He and a new girlfriend were running from the police. As Holly munched buttered popcorn, the two movie characters screamed through the countryside, the girl's legs propped against the door of their TransAm. It reminded Holly of her life with Monty and the memories overlaid those on the screen.

Holly was nineteen, working full time and going to business college. On weekends she went to bars with girlfriends. Seemed like everyone in Montana did that. It was a big thing—go to bars and dance, and she enjoyed it because she could be someone else other than shy Holly.

One night at the Jekyll and Hyde she saw a nice looking guy at the bar. "Think he'll dance with me?" she whispered to her friend.

"Sure, get his friend Corey to ask him to come over."

How embarrassed she was when he danced with someone else.

"Go on, Holly, I dare you. Talk to him. If you don't, I will. Remember the book we're reading says to be assertive," her friend teased.

Holly, feeling as if her heart would explode any minute, walked over to his table. What should she say? Somehow it was easy. He was intelligent and seemed alert. While the jukebox spun Jim Croce singing about time in a bottle, they had a wonderful time talking. Later, sitting in her car, they discovered they had things in common. Both felt rejected by parents, as if they didn't belong anywhere.

Monty had pulled his needle out of his pocket. Holly remembered feeling shocked. She'd never seen anything like that before.

He said, "I've got a drug problem, but I want to quit. Look, no more." And he threw the needle out the car window.

That was the first of a long string of promises, but she was naive and gullible.

She didn't think she would see Monty again, but he showed up at her door, reminding her of a lonely little boy, asking if she would run away with him to Seattle. He needed her, and she needed someone to belong to. She went with him.

After that, they went to Great Falls. The first morning there Monty got his needle and pack of white powder and shot up. Holly had never seen that done before. It made her nauseous to watch him.

"Want to get high with me?" he asked.

"I don't think so...well, do you really want me to?" She had hoped he would say no.

"Well, Sweetheart, why don't you try it just once? You may go for the way it feels."

"Okay," she said softly, and he filled up the needle.

She couldn't watch when he stuck it in her arm, and then her head got light, and she tingled all over. It wasn't too bad...better than marijuana, which always made her depressed. Besides, it was something the two of them could share. They might have pancakes for every meal, but they always had cocaine. And marijuana for in-between times.

No matter where they were, it was the same. Short-term jobs, scary people going in and out of their house, and always, always, at the hub of everything— drugs.

The summer after they met they learned she was pregnant. That was when Mom dangled the apartment and a car in front of Monty for marrying her daughter.

The thing was, Monty had a job and had cut way down on drugs. The two of them planned to be married, but the pressure from Mom got too much for him. One day he blew up at her mother and left.

Holly moved in with her mother. She was like a beetle she had seen once on the schoolground, tormented on each side by boys with sticks. She had felt so sorry for that beetle. After being pushed and pulled, it died. That's what would happen to her baby. Maybe it would happen to her.

After the abortion, her mother said Holly should get on with her life. Live with her and get a good secretarial job. She was so good in that field, that although she hadn't finished the course, the business college gave her a diploma and recognition for being their top student.

"But Mom," Holly said. "I want to be an airline stewardess or a model, or maybe an interior decorator. I could go to school and be on my own. I want to live my own life."

Mom was adamant. "Holly, you don't know how to live your life. Get a job and stay with me, and I'll give you a new car...any kind you want, and you spend your money on clothes."

Trapped again. Holly left the house one evening to go to a party. Monty was there. Familiar feelings surged. She loved him. Why had things worked out the way they had? They hadn't mentioned the abortion, just talked casually and she went home to cry into her pillow.

Monty called the next morning. He was in jail and needed her to post bail.

After her signature on the bond they took off for Yellowstone Park. The park had been fun. Holly, busy at work, didn't have time for drugs, except at occasional boat games and parties. She hadn't known where Monty was most of the time or what he did.

But one night he came in the cabin door and said they weren't living right and that they were leaving the park. Just like that. She had argued. She knew their way of life was against her Catholic upbringing.

Her mother had pounded that into her head, but it was safe. No commitment—no hurts. In the end she went to Phoenix with him.

Then, on top of Hoover Dam, it was a different Monty. "Marry me, or else." So she wouldn't lose him, she went along with the spur-of-the-moment marriage. It certainly hadn't been the beautiful wedding of her dreams.

The two in the movie were making the sheriff look like an idiot, but Holly wasn't paying attention. She was remembering how her mom had thought their marriage certificate had come from a joke store, and she laughed aloud during a passionate screen kiss.

Her friend elbowed her. "What's with you?"

"Sorry," Holly whispered.

She concentrated on the movie. The twosome were now eating hamburgers and discussing their relationship problems.

Hamburgers. Monty tried to go good for several months after their marriage. She was pregnant again. Then one night he said he was going out for hamburgers. He never came back.

Holly figured he had hit the bars and passed out someplace. When he did come back three days later, he was apologetic, but she knew the cycle had begun again.

THE END scrawled across the heads of the actor and actress. They headed down the highway for a carefree joyride while the sheriff threw his hat on the ground in frustration.

Holly stuffed her popcorn box under her seat, and looked at her friend. "I'm thirsty. Let's go to Jekyll's."

Tonight the memories were overwhelming. She needed to jam the reception.

8

A Shattered Melody

Holly: Summer, 1976

"Holly," Mrs. Moser called from the livingroom the next evening, "someone sent this news clipping. Listen to this. Monty Christensen...are you listening, Holly?

> Monty Christensen, twenty-two, of Missoula, Mont., was arrested three miles east of Grangeville, after a tip he was hitchhiking. He was charged with possession of narcotics with intent to deliver and grand larceny. After his arrest, officers found that he was wanted in Alburquerque for first-degree burglary. Acting on information received Monday afternoon, police entered and searched a residence on N. 7th and arrested five suspects and one juvenile in possession of drugs. However the armed-and-wanted suspect was not in the residence at the time of arrest, the biggest bust ever made by Grangeville police....

Holly raced down the hallway. "What's he doing in Grangeville?" She snatched the article from her mother's hand. "Let me read it."

"Well, go on," urged her mother.

The suspect, known as Monty Montana, had told the residents,'I'd rather die than let a cop take me, and I'll kill any cop who tries.' He was considered armed and dangerous.

She waved the clipping in the air. "Dangerous! Monty isn't dangerous."

"Keep reading, Holly."

The suspect returned to the house around midnight. The officers on stakeout moved in for the arrest. Officer Coven put a shotgun to Montana's head and told him, "Police...freeze!

Holly dropped the paper and screamed, "They were going to kill him!"

"Apparently they didn't." Her mother picked up the clipping and continued reading.

Montana leaned over the seat of a 1956 Plymouth he was stealing to escape arrest, hit the gas and took off. Officers shot out the back tires and when Montana abandoned the car, pursued him on foot. The stolen vehicle, which was believed to be carrying large quantities of narcotics, was impounded. A 1973 Cadillac was also impounded.

Mrs. Moser took off her reading glasses. "He's

done it again. I suppose the Cadillac is the one he said his grandmother gave him. Wonder why he would have to steal another car? Well, that's Monty. Be glad you're rid of him." She handed the article to Holly.

Holly crumpled it into a ball and, clutching it so tightly her nails cut into her palm, walked slowly to her bedroom. Jared slept in his crib, long dark lashes anchoring his eyelids. Holly caressed the tousled brown hair. "Nearly two years old. You're going to need a haircut soon, Kiddo," she said softly.

So many things had happened since he was born. Monty disappeared a few weeks before Jared's birth, and she lived with her mom, on welfare.

She had felt so alone. At nearly eight months pregnant, she couldn't bar-hop with her friends. Sometimes she was so desperate for fun, she'd wear a poncho, and with her hands in her pocket, hope she only looked as though her poncho were extra big.

She had also been alone the day she delivered Jared. Her mom was home laying carpet. God, how she hated aloneness, but that seemed to always be her lot.

As much as she had tried to force herself to laugh and pretend she didn't hurt, depression settled in. An iron-gray fog filled with Monty's bills, bills left from his ex-wife, hospital and doctor bills, and the resentment of being tied down with a baby.

She couldn't get hold of Monty. She didn't know where he was. When he had called three weeks later asking if they had a baby, she tried not to let him hear her hurt. She told him the baby had blue eyes, and he responded, "That's not my son." Why had he said that? It unleashed her bitterness.

When he said he wanted money to come home to see the baby, she knew he was lying. Yet she wanted to believe him, so she told him about Uncle Truman.

"In a way I'm glad I did it," she whispered to her sleeping son. "It was nice for awhile, wasn't it?" She arranged his blanket and went out, leaving the door open a crack.

"I'm going to Jekyll's, Mom," she said. "The gals are getting together."

"Holly, I want you to meet new friends, but I wish you didn't drink so much. I will say one thing for the religious fanaticism you got into—you cut way down." Her mother stroked rose fingernail polish on her nails and blew on them.

"It wasn't fanaticism." Holly closed her eyes. Her mother had made similar remarks before. "Monty and I had a close relationship with God."

She paused, remembering the time she and Monty had gone to dinner and church with his boss and got steered to the altar. The pastor had explained how Jesus knocks at the doors of our hearts, waiting to be asked in. She knew Monty didn't feel anything, but she had cried. It was as though someplace in the wilderness of her soul, a sweet chord was struck, signaling the way home. But that night she hadn't done anything except cry. It was later, with Uncle Truman that she understood.

Slowly, she said to her mother, "I guess I've always wanted an experience with God."

"But we've always been a religious family, Holly. You didn't have to go outside our church. Remember how we prayed the rosary, and you studied catechism and how you prayed to St. Anthony when you lost something?"

"I know, but St. Anthony never found my stuff." Holly bit her tongue at the look on her mother's face.

"I'm sorry, Mom, but while I memorized what God was, I never related to Him. He was in the sky—out there somewhere, but not reachable. I prayed and I knew He heard me because the catechism said so, but I never knew He always answers. I discovered He does."

"That's where you went off the deep end, Holly. We're not to worry about those things. That's the duty of the priest. To discern God's Word and tell us."

"Mom, the Bible says, 'There is one God and one mediator between God and man, the man Christ Jesus.' The verse slipped out. She hadn't read the Bible, much less quoted it, for a long time. Besides, she realized that her upbringing in thinking that priests were her mediator was an underlying factor in losing her closeness with God. She had asked Jesus to come into her life, but hadn't made Him fully master, because somehow she felt she wasn't directly responsible to God.

She sighed. She was far from that relationship and shouldn't be preaching to her mom, but if she could just explain. "Mom, when I used to go to confession once a month, I made up the amounts of times I had sinned. I thought God would punish me for that because that's what He was there for—to punish people. But I learned that He doesn't just wait around to whack people with a rolled-up newspaper. He's loving and tender and kind."

This was an uncomfortable subject. Why was she discussing something she had left behind? She wanted to end it and go, so she tried a light note. "Our church has a lot of good things about it, Mom. It's beautiful, and I still love it. Do you remember one Sunday when I was little, I looked up at the priest and blurted out loud, 'God sure dresses pretty?' " She laughed.

Mrs. Moser examined her nails. "Yes, I remember. The beauty of the sacraments and vestments, and the mass are enough for me. Why weren't you satisfied?"

Holly didn't answer for a moment. Then, thoughtfully, she said, "I guess I needed God to hug me."

* * *

Holly stood and looked at the sign as if she had never noticed it before. JEKYLL AND HYDE — A sandwich shop by day and a bar at night. Two personalities. The thoughts plaguing her on the drive downtown wouldn't let go. Why couldn't she and Monty hang on to the relationship they had with Jesus and each other? What happened? Neither of them had meant it to end like this.

Two forces in each of them battled for supremacy. Which one would ultimately win? Or would it end like the Jekyll-and-Hyde novel she read in high school—in death? She shuddered and went into the bar.

"Holly, over here." Her friends beckoned through the murk of cigarette smoke and dim light. "We ordered you a drink. Guess what we heard about Monty."

Holly arched her mouth in a smile. "Probably what I heard. He's in jail." She closed her hand around the glass in front of her. It was something to hang onto.

While the others chattered, her mind and the dance floor's strobe lights pulsated in rhythm. Why, why, why?

How she had laughed last year when her aunt called from Corvallis saying how well Monty was doing. She thought Aunt Mildred was naive. Then Monty called, giving her malarky how he was different. Something about God. All the depression she had felt since the baby was born had roared out at him. She hadn't finished berating him when she heard her uncle's soft voice.

"Holly, dear, it may be hard for you to understand, but Monty didn't have to change or do good things before God accepted him. God's Word says we are saved through faith by God's own graciousness. It is a *gift* of God. Then, *He* starts the changes. Honey, you can do the same thing."

Holly remembered the night she cried at the altar. The same longing awakened. "Yes, Uncle Truman, I'd like that."

She prayed the sinner's prayer with him, hung up the phone, and ran to her bedroom. Kneeling at the foot of her bed, the tears flowed. All kinds of tears. Sorrowful ones for the way she had lived, happy tears, tears of deep love. When they had spent themselves, she felt refreshed, clean. Jesus was real. He had done a work inside her.

"Bartender! We need another round." Her friend's voice jarred Holly back to the smoke and confusion.

"Holly, you've hardly touched your drink. Get with it."

"She's pining over Monty," said another.

"No, I'm not," Holly laughed. "He's out of my life for good." She sipped her vodka. Somehow tonight, it didn't taste good.

"Hey, Holly, wanna dance?"

"Sure, Corey."

The strobes alternated colors in chaotic patterns. Holly giggled. "It looks like Dr. Spock is beaming us up."

"What?" shouted Corey. "Too bad about Monty," he yelled.

Holly shrugged her shoulders to the beat. The whole world seemed to know.

Corey did a fancy turn. "Heard he was religious for awhile." He laughed. "Maybe he'll get on his knees and *repent*, and you'll go running back. Right, Holly? Holly, what's the matter?"

Holly left him standing on the dance floor, picked up her purse, and stormed out the door. Monty had made her into a laughing stock. Was that what everyone thought—that she fell for all his lines and kept running back like a faithful dog?

She slammed her car door and gunned the engine. Of course she had. The night she had accepted Jesus—maybe she should have left it that way. But she had been so pleased when Monty told her he had a spot for them in the Corvallis countryside because he knew she liked the country. He had thought about her. That was a factor in her going back to him.

Then when he met six-week-old Jared and her at the airport, he seemed different. He teared up when he saw the baby. He was a sensitive person. Had that all been a line? Yes...no. He just had trouble hanging on to anything. And if she were honest with herself, she had problems too.

She had so many things to get used to. So many changes. It was like the song she had heard once and had written down because it fit her teenage feelings.

Changes coming down for a long time,
Changes coming down on me,
Can't seem to carry them all now,

Been wishin' there was someone else I could be.
Oh, now, who really cares; oh, won't somebody
listen,
Let me say what's on my mind.
Can I tell it all to you? I need someone to
talk to,
And no one will spare me the time.

In Corvallis there was no one to talk to about her confusion. She had a new baby and was far from home. Uncle Truman and Aunt Mildred were wonderful but even with as much hostility as there was between her and her mother, Holly missed her.

And Monty—Monty really was different. He was gung-ho for Jesus. He had had a mountain-top experience, and he was walking tall and talking tall. He led a co-worker to the Lord. She was proud of him. She felt he knew absolutely everything about spiritual life.

She also had an experience with the Lord, but compared to Monty's, it didn't seem like much. She said to the pastor or someone from their Bible class, "I don't know if I'm really a Christian."

"Well, Holly, if you feel that way, maybe you didn't really accept the Lord before. Now pray with me...."

And then the doubts set in again, and she would repeat the scenario. She was embarrassed because Monty was everybody's fair-haired boy, and look at her problems.

The new Monty was also confusing. As bad as it

had been before, she knew him. She knew his weaknesses and where he probably was during a late night. Now she didn't.

"Monty, it's midnight."

"I know, Sweetheart. I was witnessing to some of the guys and forgot about time. I'm sorry."

Witnessing. Telling about his experience with Jesus. But at this hour?

"Umm, were there any women there?" she casually asked.

When he denied it, she wasn't convinced.

At first she loved the Friday night home groups that sometimes lasted 'til after midnight with the music and talk. But there were times they couldn't get a babysitter, so Monty would go and she stayed home.

Soon she withdrew to her old shy self, wondering if some of the outgoing "spiritual" women appealed to Monty. When she dwelled on those thoughts, they invariably came out of her mouth dripping with bitterness and insecurity.

"Monty, do you wish I were more like Cathy?" Or, baiting him..."I'll bet your friends feel sorry for you, married to me."

Monty told her she was off base and that made it worse. They argued and neither knew what to do about it.

Corey's words, "—and you'll go running back,"

came to her.

"No, Corey," she said aloud, "I won't go back to that. I've forgiven him for the last time." She gripped the steering wheel tighter.

Crossing the bridge over the Yellowstone River, Holly turned the Mustang toward the yellow sandstone rimrocks that looked over the Billings valley. All-night markets and gas stations surrendered to river-irrigated pastures and comfortable farm houses. At the upward edge of the pastures, rabbit brush staked a claim, then tall sage and twisted pine trees.

How many times had she come up here to the old Indian cliffs? First to girl scout camp, then to high school keggers. A couple of times in desperate loneliness and confusion, she had come to stare at suicide cliff where the Indians used to force herds of buffalo over the edge.

Holly stopped the car. Across the valley, the sun's gold-bound crimson border dropped behind the foothills.

She gazed at it until the spot turned cold and the sun's warmth wasn't for her anymore. For someone else. That's the way love had always been in her life. Out of reach.

When she and Monty were in Oregon, she remembered watching the church people smile at her. The smiles included Monty and her as Christians, but they lived in an inner circle where the sun always shone.

Those Christians grew up in the church and married someone who also grew up in the church. Their lives revolved around family and church meetings. They had never had contact with Monty's and Holly's world, or with people like Monty and Holly.

So Holly pressed her nose against the window envying their warmth and interaction, and sometimes received a few rays of sunny smiles. How could she share with them her struggles with unforgiveness and bitterness and resentment? They never had them, so they wouldn't understand. And she might risk losing the smiles.

However, over the weeks, those rays paled as Monty's and her struggles became apparent to everyone. She heard the whispers.

"They're just weak."

"Do you think they really are Christians? You can't be a Christian and continue to smoke. Someone saw him smoking."

"I didn't know Holly had an abortion. Glad you told me. In the Wednesday meeting, let's pray she asks for forgiveness."

Others in the church encouraged and tried to reach out to them, but it was too late. She and Monty daily grew weaker and had not the strength to lift their hands for help. The whispers and frowns added the final blows. The sweet melody hadn't lasted forever. God let her down. Monty let her down. She didn't want either of them anymore. Could she ever find the sun again?

Holly bent her head on the steering wheel. Sobs shook her body until, exhausted, she fell asleep.

A knock on the window startled her awake. A blue uniformed sheriff looked in. His police car was alongside hers, its light and radio noise broadcasting into the quiet night.

"Ma'am."

Holly straightened her stiff back and rolled down her window.

"Ma'am, are you all right?"

"Yes, Officer." She realized that her mascara must be all over her face and her eyes probably puffy.

"Well, it isn't safe for you out here at midnight. You drive on down the hill and I'll follow you."

Holly obediently retraced the route to town. The police car turned off, and she drove home, musing that it was the earliest she'd gotten in for awhile.

* * *

When the alarm went off, an aching browness coated the area behind her closed eyelids—the kind of headache that wouldn't reach its crescendo until late in the day. She had better stay home from work. At least it isn't from a hangover, she grimly thought to herself, as she buried her head in the pillow.

The next time she awakened, it was noon. A note was taped to her door.

> Holly, you were groaning in your sleep, so decided not to wake you. Took Jared to nursery school.
>
> Mom

Holly wandered into the kitchen, reheated the coffee, and swallowed a couple of aspirins. The doorbell chimed.

"Good morning," said the mailman. "Hoped someone would be home. Package for Mrs. Moser."

Holly thanked him and closed the door. The bell sounded again.

"Sorry," said the mailman. "Almost forgot this." He handed her an envelope addressed to Holly Christensen. The return address was M. Christensen, Grangeville, Idaho.

9

Ring Around the Rosy

Holly: Fall, 1976

Monty! Holly took the envelope in her thumb and forefinger and dropped it in the wastebasket.

No more playing on her sympathies. No more expecting her to help him. He and his letter could stay where they were—in the can. She waggled her head in appreciation of her witticism and was immediately sorry. Pain thudded against her forehead.

She spread blackberry jam on a slice of toast and smiled. They had fun making trails through the blackberry thickets in Oregon. When they met each other in the middle, Monty would pop an especially sweet berry in her mouth. A loneliness settled around her heart, its ache rivaling that in her head.

She walked back in the living room and retrieved the letter. Taking a deep breath, she tore it open and unfolded a packet of papers. One was the same article she had received. There was another newspaper clipping describing the shootout more fully. Holly couldn't stand to read more than a paragraph. Monty had nearly been killed.

Underneath was a letter from Monty. "Dear Holly, Surprise!" He went on to tell her what led to the shootout.

And Holly, while I sat in jail, I figured what a mess I've made of things, including our lives. I asked to see a pastor and told him everything I've done. I told him I wanted to give my heart back to Jesus.

I could tell he thought I was conning him, but he told me Christ would forgive me again if I asked Him and if I changed the direction I was going. So I did. You may be so mad at me you won't want to read this, and I don't blame you. Just wanted you to know what happened.

Love to Jared—Monty

Holly threw the letter back in the basket. The same old Monty. The same old stuff. Like a childhood game where everyone danced around a person who was "it." When that person fell down, everyone else did, too. And they began again. Around and around.

She got her car keys. She'd pick up Jared early from playschool.

* * *

Two days later, Mrs. Moser handed Holly another letter. "Ordinarily, I wouldn't want you to read this, but I'm curious about what happened. Here."

Holly opened the envelope and for her mother's benefit, read in a sing-song voice.

Dear Holly,

I hope you don't mind too much hearing from me again. I'm writing this from the "tiger cage." That's a half-inch steel cage inside a cell. Double security for dangerous guys like me. It's a hot summer, and believe me, it's terrible inside this box, but other than that, I feel good.

Holly's voice faltered. She stopped sing-songing and read quietly,

I didn't offer the authorities any information. They figured I was hauling large quantities of drugs, so they took the Cadillac apart, piece by piece. But after I turned my life back to Jesus, I felt God wanted me to straighten things out, so I told them I did have cocaine and told them where I threw it out the car window.

They said, "We looked and couldn't find it. Take us there."

They shackled and handcuffed me and took me to the place where I had thrown it on someone's lawn. The people had run over it with a lawn mower. There was nothing but the wrapping. Can you believe it? The upshot was that they had no chargeable substance, so they had to drop the drug charges. Isn't that something?

Of course they have me on intent to deliver and grand larceny because the kid I told you about charged me with stealing his car. He didn't want his folks to know he was in on it. My two ounces of pot would have made a misdemeanor—no jail term, but they thought the kid's two ounces were mine, too. And four make a felony. So I've been sentenced to three years in the Idaho penitentiary. The Eldorado was sold at a police auction.

I'm not proud of myself and don't mean to make this into a "poor-me" letter, but thought you'd want to know. Love, Monty

P.S. Great things are happening. Tell you later.

"Well, we don't want to know. You aren't going to answer that, are you Holly?" Mrs. Moser jabbed her finger toward the offending letter.

"No, Mom, I certainly won't. He's made his own bed." But Holly couldn't help looking twice at the "love."

* * *

The following day Holly grabbed the mail before her mother saw it. She wasn't sure why, but she wanted this to be private. She went to her bedroom, propped against the headboard and read,

Dear Holly,

I can't believe what's going on. Everyone who comes in my jail cell gets saved. A kid came in on a D.W.I. and he stepped through the door and right away said, "I don't know what you've got, but I want it."

And I said, "It's Jesus."

He said, "I used to know the Lord. I turned my back on Him."

When I asked him if he would like to invite Jesus back in, he broke. The power of God was magnificent.

And then comes a guy who's in for murder. He had been in both the Korean War and in 'Nam. Killed a lot of people, so when he got out, he got in the kill-for-hire business. The last contract didn't work, so he's put in with me.

Holly, his eyes were cold and damp looking. And he said to me, "I'm going to kill you."

Well, I'd been reading a book about how somebody facing death said, "Praise God, this is graduation day. I get to go to Heaven." So I just sat there thinking about that. And because I didn't react, he kind of goes bananas...and you know what? He started telling me the story of his life. For a week I counseled him, and he poured it all out, about the mutilation he's seen. He told me all the reasons God can't forgive him.

So one day I decided it was time to tell him about Jesus. I said, "If you'll ask Him into your heart, He'll fill that hole in your life. God loves you so much. He planned for you to come to this jail and talk to me so you could receive Him as your personal Savior and Lord. Well, he sat there with a funny look, and I thought, oh boy, that was a mistake.

All of a sudden, the kid at the other end of our chow table rolled off the bench onto the floor and started bawling. He said, "That's what I've needed all my life. I want it."

I said to the murderer, "Excuse me, please." And I marched the kid to his cell and led him to Jesus. Opened my Bible to John and told him to start reading. Then I went back to the first guy, and he said, "Pray for me, will ya?"

Holly, I prayed, and then I felt strange. Something was wrong. I turned his face to me and...I thought he had died. You could tell by his eyes he wasn't in his body. Boy, I was scared, and I started praying in a panic.

After a couple of minutes, "kerpowww." He came up as though he dived in the water and came back up to the surface. He exploded, "Jesus forgave me! He set me free! I saw Him! He took me out of my body, back to my old neighborhood to show me everyone He wants me to tell about Him."

I didn't know what was going on. Seven days before, this guy's going to kill me...and now.

Anyway, those are two out of the six who've been with me and got saved. God's doing great things.

I hired an attorney and he said, "Monty, you're more free in there than I am out here."

Please write. I love you and Jared.

There was another letter from a pastor in Grangeville recounting the things Monty said.

I have witnessed the biggest revival that this town has seen. It's unbelievable, but more people are being saved in Monty's jail cell than in the entire town in all the years I've been here.

Monty thinks you won't believe him, so he asked me to write. By the way, he would appreciate hearing from you. God's best to you and your son....

Holly folded the letter. God really had His hand on Monty. It was awesome.

Well, maybe she would drop him a note to encourage him. But not today. She enjoyed her freedom too much. Didn't she?

*   *   *

"Yes, Holly is here, but she doesn't want to speak to you." Holly looked up in surprise at her mother's phone conversation.

"I know you're Monty's pastor, but Holly is trying to make a new life. She doesn't need...."

"I'll take it, Mom." Holly took the receiver from her angry mother. "Hello, Pastor."

"Holly, I thought I would tell you how much Monty appreciated your note the other day. He really has changed from what I gather he was. I pray you'll give him a chance. Maybe you two can get back together. Do you know what happened today?" The minister went to on tell about more miracles.

Holly tapped her foot impatiently. "Mmm, isn't that something. Yes, well, I'll see. Good-bye."

"Holly, you'd better not get mixed up with him again." Her mother wagged a finger in Holly's face. "Because I won't help you out again."

Holly didn't answer. She went to her bedroom and lay down, staring at the ceiling. Did her lack of responsiveness to Monty mean she was trying to get back at him? Dangle him and have her freedom too, just as he had? Hurt him? Pay him back? She got up and took her wedding ring out of a box and stared at it for a long time.

Monty was a special person. If she wanted to keep him for whatever reason, she had better do something. She got out her prettiest stationery and began to write.

Dear Monty,

As I said in my letter, I was shook hearing what happened to you. But I'm sure it's for a reason.

You're not dangerous. You're a man who has been hurt and rejected through life. I remember the time I found you at your folks' place, sleeping on a board in the pigpen because they wouldn't allow you in the house. My heart broke. You are sensitive and loving and need to be accepted and understood.

You tried hard in the past to provide for the family and be a good husband. Sometimes you got frustrated and felt inadequate.

This is a quote from Peter Marshall: "We are souls living in bodies; therefore when we fall in love, it isn't just physical attraction. If it is, it won't last. God opens our eyes to let us see someone else's soul. We fall in love with the inner person—the person who will live forever. That's why God is the greatest asset to romance. He thought it up in the first place. Include Him in every part of your marriage, and He will lift it above the level of the mundane to something rare and beautiful and lasting."

I talked to the pastor and he told me to keep the hope of you and me and fully trust the Lord. God can perform miracles. Love, Holly

She read over what she had written. A warmth she hadn't felt for nearly a year glowed inside her. It shocked her.

I guess it's true, she said to herself. I still love him. She folded the letter and placed it in the envelope. God will have to perform a miracle. Especially in me.

10

State Prison

Monty: Fall, 1976

I tossed and turned on the thin mattress. I shouldn't have asked the pastor to call Holly the other day. She hated to be bugged and he said her mom was mad. Why was I pushing to get our relationship back? Her brief note was friendly, but not anything you'd call loving. Why should it be?

I opened my eyes. Chrome colored light slanted into the cell like an advance guard, announcing the approach of something big. The ex-killer-for-hire snored softly.

It was a new day, one that God made and planned. He was in charge of my life whether or not Holly and I got back together. I reached for my Bible, shaking my head. The old enemy sure liked to do his dirty work on my mind at night. If I stopped to realize that, I would have had more sleep.

The marker was in the first chapter of First Corinthians.

...For Christ did not send me to baptize, but to preach the gospel, not in cleverness of speech.... For the word of the cross is to those who are perishing, foolishness, but to us who are saved, it is the power of God. (I Cor. 1:17,18)

I put down the Bible and sat thinking about what I read. As I looked at the wall, a picture in sharp focus appeared—a cowboy on a horse, riding across a desolate prairie. Behind him was a city, his family and comfort. He rode beside a tree-lined river. I realized I was seeing the same type of vision I had seen in Corvallis, a movie that allowed me to absorb every detail in a split second.

This time I could almost hear with my ears the Lord's voice, "Monty, you are just now entering the vast frontier of My Word."

I looked to see if my cell-mate saw what I did, but he slept on. All kinds of feelings surged through me—fright, awe, excitement. I lay on my face and for the next two hours, released them in tears.

"God, You get me out of this mess, and I'll go to Bible college and will serve You all my life."

"Hey, Man, what's going on?" My cell-mate looked at me wide-eyed.

"It's okay," I said, pulling on my coveralls. "The Lord just told me something about my life, and it's overwhelming."

"Letter for you, Christensen." The guard threw down a pale-blue envelope from Holly. I tore it open, and the tears started again as I could almost hear her voice, "Keep the hope of you and me and fully trust the Lord. God can perform miracles. Love."

I touched the letter to my lips. God already performed a tiny one.

The guard opened the door again. "Your sentence came through, Christensen. They're shippin' you to the pen in Boise. Pack up." He handed me a bar of soap and a razor and watched while I scraped at the dry lather.

This was fast. No time to write Holly. I turned to my cell-mate. "Listen, when the pastor comes in, tell him to notify Holly where I am, but I don't want her coming up to see me. I couldn't stand her seeing me there."

"Sure, Monty." He gave me a quick bear hug. "You'll never know what you've meant to me. I can hold up my head and I know God's going to do something with my life. Thanks."

The guard chained my feet together, wrapped a chain around my waist, and clamped on handcuffs. He looped a chain from those to the waist chain of another guy who was chained to another. With small steps, we headed for the van.

* * *

"Here's your bedding, Christensen." The Boise prison guard handed me a three-inch foam mattress, sheets and a blanket. "It's September and gets cold here soon. Use this army jacket." He started to leave. "You're in a close-custody unit, if you didn't know it. We're not letting a guy like you roam around. You get out at chow time. That's all."

Oh well, I thought. I won't be here long. After that vision I made God a promise. I knew He'd honor it.

All of us "bad guys" were isolated in one wing of the prison. The days dragged, but at night, although the wing was closed, they let us keep our cell doors open. I wandered in and out talking about the Lord.

The men were like kindling, dry, and in place. All that was needed was the spark of the Holy Spirit to ignite the flame. And flame that wing did. Men accepted Jesus; they learned to worship. We got a Bible study going and had a prayer time when we prayed for our families.

The prison was tough. It wasn't uncommon to see five or more guys ganging up on one man, beating him until he was dead or nearly so. Or the same number would gang up and force a man to homosexual acts. I hadn't been there long before I heard the statistics—at least three killings a year.

The guards in our unit matched the inmates, mean and tough. They had a lousy job and a lousy attitude toward life in general and me in particular. Somehow I threatened them. I could tell it and steered clear as much as possible.

One day a guard yanked me out of my cell. He pushed me to a concrete room where the mop buckets and heavy-duty brooms with metal handles were kept. My insides turned buttery. This was no outing, but what had I done? I always said hello to him and did everything he told me.

He locked the door and backed me into a corner. "You're nothin' but a two-bit liar punk," he hissed. "You're a no-good con man. Usin' this Jesus stuff to get out of here."

This guy's crazy, I thought.

He unscrewed a metal mop handle and raised it over his head. There was no way out. I'd be beaten to a bloody pulp. And then he'd say it was my fault, and I'd wind up doing a thirty-day stint in the maximum-security hole. This was it.

But suddenly, starting from the bottom of my feet and swelling up through my body and out my mouth, came, "I love the Lord my God more than my mom, my wife, my family. I love the Lord my God more than I love my life."

As the last word rolled off my tongue, the guard fell back, dropping the mop handle. He quickly unlocked the door and ushered me out.

I wasn't sure what had happened, but I knew God intervened. In the mail that day was a letter from Holly.

Monty,

I've been having nightmares almost every night. Last night I woke up screaming. I dreamed someone in prison harmed you and you died. It was terrifying.

When I came to my senses, it calmed me to know that the Lord is watching over you. He has helped me pray and be honest with Him. I can hardly wait to attend church Sunday. I'll continue to pray for you.

My love, Holly

Had there been a tie-in with my experience with the guard? The only thing I knew for certain was that the Lord was indeed performing miracles.

* * *

"Watch out, here comes Crazy Mushroom."

Crazy Mushroom glided across the prison yard, hands over his head like a tent. "Guess what I am. I'm a kite. I'm higher than a kite. Here, you want to be, too?" He reached into his pocket and pulled out a mangled puffball.

I shook my head. "Mushroom, those don't work. They're ordinary ones."

"Oh, no." He shook his head and whispered, "And I'm the only one who knows." He "flew" away.

I watched him, remembering the patients in the state mental institution. That's where Mushroom belonged. What snag in the system put him here? But the system did foul up at times. Reform school had been proof.

* * *

A couple of months later, the decision came from the top. Christensen was to go to Cottonwood, the minimum security prison.

The day I left, I said goodbye to the guard who had tried to attack me. Since that day, he'd gone out of his way to avoid me, and this was no exception. He vanished around a corner.

I couldn't find a single Christian at Cottonwood, so each night I lay in bed and imagined laying hands on the inmates, and prayed for God to save them. I did that by the hour until when I talked to them about the Lord, they were ready. Eventually, many came to Jesus.

Two months later I got word that the state of Montana wanted me in court on the forgery charge and that Idaho would extradite me as soon as arrangements were made, but I had to wait in Grangeville. I went with two deputies in a twin engine airplane. Still shackled and still handcuffed, but in style.

For three weeks I sat in the Grangeville jail. The

waiting was getting to me. Why was God stretching this out? It was also discouraging Holly.

Dear Monty,

I haven't been following the Lord, and I feel uncomfortable around Christians. I've meant to go to church and change my life, but am scared of all the questions—"Where's your husband?—Are you married?"

I feel like a failure for being divorced—a failure in the church, a failure as a woman. So here I am, hiding.

I'm probably the wrong companion for you. My life has been so meaningless, so frustrated, so lonely. It's almost unbearable to try and make it through another day.

Mom told Jared that she had peeked in his room while he was napping. He said he wished she wouldn't do that because he was dreaming about his daddy and didn't want to wake up until it was over because he likes to dream about his daddy....

I read the last part of the letter twice, then lay on my bunk and draped a towel over my face. "What have I done to my family?" I groaned. "I wish I could do it all over." I jammed the towel down harder to muffle the sound of my crying.

* * *

"Monty Christensen, you are charged with forging a five-thousand dollar check on your grandmother's account." The Montana judge scowled at me. "Do you plead guilty?"

"Yes, your Honor, but if I could be paroled, I promise to go back to Idaho and work in the Teen Challenge program," I said. Over a month ago I had talked to the Idaho leader. Besides working with them, I knew Teen Challenge could help me with my drug problem and give me some space before jumping back into the world.

The judge tapped his pen on the desk. "It's a good program. All right, you are hereby sentenced to three years. Deferred, *if* you make restitution. We'll make up a payment schedule for you. Good luck."

My heart leaped. Luck? It was God, performing another miracle.

I caught the next bus to Lewiston and Teen Challenge, and spent the hours saying to myself, everything is working out. It's working out.

I walked into the T.C. office. "Well, here I am," I said. "Sooner than we thought."

The leader looked at me in surprise. "I don't know how you did it, but if anyone could...I'm sorry, but if you came here to stay...we don't have room. Maybe later, if you get your act together and prove you're on the up and up."

I was stunned. It had seemed so right. Where was I to go? I'd better tell the judge and the parole officer.

When I did, the judge said, "You've been released on the forgery charge, so get a job."

Easier said than done, but I didn't wait around. I went to Billings, camped with my stepsister and brother-in-law, and saw Holly and Jared every night.

Holly's mom had a fit when she heard us discussing remarriage. "Neither of you has the sense of a scarecrow. If you put me through that again, I wash my hands. I will not help you. Holly, you will give me back the Mustang."

And the following week when Holly returned from work, her belongings were on her mother's front porch.

Holly charged over to see me. "What shall I do?"

"Let's get married right now," I said.

"Monty, I want a real wedding this time. Let's wait for a month. I can live with friends."

"Sweetheart, we can't keep putting it off. We're a family and need to be together, *now*."

She gave in, and I asked the local pastor if he would marry us.

"No, in my denomination I can't, Monty. You were divorced before, weren't you?"

"Yes, at eighteen."

"So I'm sorry I can't marry you two, but you and Holly and Jared move in with us until you find a minister who will marry you. I know it is tempting just to live together in the meantime, but wisdom means not giving anyone a reason to point a finger at you."

We found a pastor and a chapel. Now we needed witnesses. Holly asked her mom.

"Absolutely not. Please reconsider."

I asked my mom. "No." I asked my sister. "No."

Finally Holly got a co-worker to stand up with us. We bought real wedding rings—two for fifty dollars and had a candlelit service. Holly was more beautiful than she was the first time.

My wife and son were back; I had an application in at a Bible college.

"The good times are here," I whispered to Holly after the ceremony.

The old enemy must have heard me and gave his demons instructions.

11

Old Tapes - Old Patterns

Monty: Fall, 1977

Holly and I had arrived. We both had good-paying jobs, were going to church, and having fun watching Jared grow. On weekends we all went fishing. If we didn't catch anything, we'd buy steaks and mushrooms and cook them on the hibachi. We not only had the world by its tail, we were swinging it around our heads.

"Here, Monty." Holly handed me an envelope from the Bible college to which I had applied.

Excitedly I tore it open. "They've accepted me!" I whirled her around. "We can be out of here fast."

We looked at each other, and I knew we thought the same thing. For the first time in our lives, we lived a good life. For the first time the bills were paid with a little left over. We would have to leave all this to uproot and live on...what?

I said slowly, "Tell you what we'll do. We'll put

this off for now and keep on working. When we have a cushion of about ten thousand dollars, then I'll go to Bible college."

I saw the sparkle come back in Holly's eyes. "Good," she said. "It's not like we're giving up the idea, just postponing it."

I put the letter in the desk drawer. I knew I had made a promise to God, and I really wasn't turning my back on it. Like Holly said, just putting it off for awhile.

* * *

For the next two months, we carved our personal niches into the good life. Then one afternoon my construction boss said, "Monty, I'm having financial problems, and although you're a good foreman, today is your last day."

I walked home feeling as though I had been hit in the stomach by a Mack truck.

Holly was optimistic. "Don't worry. You'll find something else. We have to trust and be patient."

But construction had a bad year, and no one was hiring. I couldn't find any kind of work, and it didn't take long for the absence of my paycheck to be felt in the mounting stack of bills.

As in the past, whenever we had financial problems, Holly and I bickered.

"Holly, look at these bills. Why did you buy this stuff? You don't seem to get it through your head that I'm out of work!"

"They were on sale, and we needed them. And I'll pay for them out of my salary. Anyway, it looks like I'll get a raise. The company got a new computer today, and I was chosen to run it. In fact the boss said they would send me to the company branches in the Northwest and California to train others in running that type of computer. Isn't that great?"

"Great," I mumbled. "Really great." I left the room.

"Well, you could be happy about it. At least I'm bringing in money!" she called after me.

Job, the man of many troubles, said, "What I feared has happened to me." I sure related to that. Maybe I knew that Satan pushes our fears in our faces to get us discouraged and depressed, but I didn't know what to do about it.

Once again I failed. I failed my family, other people's expectations, and secretly I felt I failed God by not accepting the Bible-school offer. I hadn't learned to deal with and eliminate my old habits and patterns that contributed to my problems, in either job or marriage. And I hadn't yet learned the right thinking to replace them. So at our once-a-week prayer group, the pastor and his wife and a couple of others spent a lot of time listening to Holly and me vent our frustrations.

"Yeah, it's nice about Holly's promotion," I said.

"But I never see her anymore. She's at the office until midnight."

Holly glared. "Well, I can't help it. When we have a big work load, I've got to get it out on the computer. I have responsibility. Seems like Monty could be understanding. I can't just walk off the job if it gets tough."

The next day, without anything else to do, I was in the pastor's office. "I know I'm not supposed to be working a regular job. God wants me to preach. It's discouraging." And I would tell him again about my visions.

"Well, Monty, maybe God does want you to preach. Someday you'll be back working in the jails and with young people."

His answer about someday didn't satisfy me, and I sank deeper into the muck of depression. Then the headaches hit. Terrible, excruciating. Holly took me to the doctor.

"You've been on cocaine," he pronounced after examining me. "Your sinuses are completely burned out. There's nothing I can do except give you a shot of Demerol for the pain. Unfortunately, you'll have to come back every four hours for another shot."

"Anything, Doctor," I pleaded. "Just stop the pain."

The injection did its work. I flew out of the office laughing. It was wonderful. Holly drove home and four hours later drove me back when the effects wore off.

For nearly a week we kept up the routine, and then the doctor switched to pills. But I was already hooked on the high-voltage shots, and the pills didn't help. In desperation I bought syringes and tried to shoot the Demerol. But it didn't work. The Demerol had the same effect as heroin. Each time I took it, I had to vomit—sometimes blood. The headaches eased, but my narcotic craving was back in full force.

If the doctor wouldn't give me anymore, I knew who would. I went to see an old friend and bummed a joint.

"Come on down to Jekyll's and catch up on the scene," he coaxed.

It was something to do.

* * *

It's easy to picture Satan's hit men doubling over in laughter. They hadn't made me do anything. Although this time prescription drugs reactivated my addiction, I could have asked for help. But the drugs numbed my depression. That's how I had always dealt with it in the past. I hadn't deprogrammed my old nature. Through years of practice, the right buttons were easy to push.

After the drug button, came the button spinning the time-worn lies, "You blew your Christian walk again...you just can't make it...you can't face God...He's tired of the same old routine of sin and forgive, sin and forgive...He's tired of you...no, that prickly feeling inside you isn't from God. Ignore it. Turn your head and go your way. Don't think about it."

And I bought it—again. The lies were on high amp, and they combined with my high decibel pride about again telling God I was sorry. Together they drowned out the stirring to get right with God, the gentle voice that said He would meet me more than half way.

The button with the dollar sign hit the jackpot. I could make big bucks agenting for guys who had a free-base kitchen. Base was going for several thousand a pound and I could get a percentage of the contract. Small at first, but working up to a larger amount.

One night at Jekyll's a young blondie gazed into my bleary eyes. "I'll bet you're one of the big dealers," she cooed.

"I do all right," I said. "I front for a kitchen."

Her nose wrinkled. "Oh, you're just a middle-man." She turned to another guy.

"Hey, wait," I grabbed at the next thought in my head. "I'm also in business for myself."

She turned back, all smiles. As she chattered, I thought, why not? Why should those guys get all the money? All I need is one sale.

The next day I set up a contract for half a pound. Money up front.

"I'll bring the stuff tomorrow," I promised.

Ten thousand in cash. There in my hand. Prepare to bail out fast, I laughed to myself, as I headed for an airline ticket office. Where should I go? Seattle? No, that would be the first place the pigeons would look for me. Oregon? They wouldn't think I had connections there. And somehow, there was a longing to go back to Corvallis. See Uncle Truman. Maybe just touching the area might get rid of the unsettled, unhappy feeling inside me.

I left the ticket office and laughed again. Last time I headed down there for help, I went in a Cadillac. This time, a plane. Guess I was going up in the world.

Holly was the next problem. I didn't have the guts to tell her what I did and that she might be visited by some mad people. I also didn't have the guts to tell her good-bye again. I'd call her when I was out of town. And I'd feel guilty leaving her without money. She was home when I got there.

"Monty, where have you been for the last two days?"

"Here and there, Babe. Listen, I gotta go out again, but I brought this for you." I folded one thousand dollars and stuffed it under the couch cushion. "Buy some new tires for the car."

"Monty...."

"Give Jared a kiss for me. See you later."

* * *

Spring, 1978

Outside the Portland airport, someone pushed a
tract in my hand. I glanced at the first page.

A son took a trip to a distant land, and there
wasted all his money on parties and prostitutes....

It was the story Jesus told. The Prodigal Son. The
story I retold to people I tried to win to Christ. I
crumpled the paper and let it drop to the sidewalk.
Then I laughed aloud. That dude no doubt bought a
horse for cruising. What would he have thought if he
could have had the motor home I just rented? Instant
party.

The trouble was, I had no time to replenish my
cocaine supply before leaving Billings. Party time
would depend on if I could buy some here.

Feeling like a barge trying to maneuver around a
bunch of rowboats, I drove into the city's pit, the skid
road. I selected a bar and went in to drink until I
could spot a connection.

It was a biker's club, but I needed coke too badly
to be scared. I saw my contact. Thin, pale, hyper. A
speed freak.

I walked over to him and said, "You know where
I can get coke. Take me there and I'll give you half."

The guy flipped. "Hey, Man, get back or I bust
your head with this cue stick."

I tried a soothing voice. "Hey, I'm no cop. I've got

to have some dope." Out of the corner of my eye I saw fat, bearded bikers, spitting through the gaps in their teeth, circle me. I had walked into this one. My cut-up body would be dumped in the alley. But all of a sudden, the long-haired, pasty-faced guy said, "Okay."

I expelled a long breath and realized I was sweating. Did the prodigal son have close calls like that?

Loaded with cocaine, money, and false I.D. so I couldn't be traced, I invited my new friend and a couple of others to tour Oregon in my motor home. A new world made of money opened as we partied our way, leaving one hundred dollar tips at fancy restaurants.

We rented a small plane and flew around the area. All of us were high on cocaine, including the pilot.

I forgot about Holly. Besides, if I called her, she might accidentally tip off someone where I was. I forgot all about Truman. This was a fantastic life.

The money dwindled. I was down to fifteen hundred when I remembered the furniture Holly and I put in storage. I got it out and furnished an apartment, trying to maintain the new life-style.

It wasn't long until money and cocaine were gone. I sold the furniture. That money was soon gone. That was when I met Marcy.

She knew me by my new identity and took me home to her parents. In my spaced-out mind, the past was gone. I *was* the other guy, and I gave her parents a story about working two jobs to try to get ahead and that I loved their daughter and wanted to marry her.

"That's wonderful, Joe," they said. "Here's a hundred to tide you over until payday."

The money went for booze and cocaine, as did each paycheck I got at my car-salesman job. The past repeated itself in my relationship with the girl. I'd be gone for two and three days at a time—loaded or passed out someplace. Marcy was angry. Her parents were angry. Things were going downhill.

One night, while driving the dealership's demo-car, bombed out of my tree, I drove through town at one-hundred-fifteen miles an hour, lost control and spun out. The fact that I wasn't killed was a miracle that didn't register right away. The cops took me in and gave me a ticket on the false I.D.

Anyone going that speed has to be suspicious, and the police did some weeding in the I.D. files. They came up with Monty Christensen, on parole.

I got word and split to another town. With no money, I lived with hippies and did anything to stay high. Beg, borrow—or steal.

The jewelry department in the town's shopping mall had nice rings.

"I'd like to buy that one," I said to the clerk. "May I try it on?" I admired it on my finger, and while he watched, walked out, and took off running.

I knew the clerk gave the security cops a full description of me, as did the person who saw me burglarizing a house. I realized I was wanted for using false I.D., using a stolen driver's license, parole violation, as well as the burglary and strong arm theft of the ring. And the police not only were onto me, they wanted me, bad.

One morning as I left the house where I was staying and walked across the street to have breakfast with friends, police surrounded my house. I escaped out the friend's back door.

I ran in a blind panic. The police were only a step behind.

So why, as I dodged from house to house, did two Bible stories keep coming to me? The Prodigal Son. Things were so bad for him he tried to get the pigs' garbage food away from them. Guess that's were I was. Rock bottom. Vying with other skid-roaders for food or money to stay drunk.

I heard a sermon once about the other story. A man had a demon in him. The demon left, but the man didn't replace him with anything. He was like an empty house. The demon came back bringing seven others worse than he, and they all entered the man, and the poor guy was worse than before. It hadn't made a lot of sense then. Maybe now I was beginning to understand it.

I was in a constant state of drug overdosing. With the overdosing came insanity. I did things I never thought possible, like going after a guy with a knife.

"Stop him! Call the police!" the bystanders shouted.

The chase was over. Within minutes the cops mobbed me. They jerked my arm so hard it separated from its socket, put the cuffs on me, and proceeded to beat and choke me until I passed out.

I was unconscious for two and a half days and awakened in the jail's psychiatric unit, still out of my head. Later I was told that I screamed to be let out of there. Three orderlies descended on me but with superhuman strength, I slugged all three, and ran through the hospital.

"Get that raging maniac under confinement," they ordered.

When I really came to, I was strapped to a bed. Because of the beating, I couldn't talk for a couple of days. During that time I thought fast. They knew who I was, and given a little time would find all the charges against me. It was back to prison for a lot of years. I had to get out of there. But how?

When I was able to talk, I went to the head of the clinic. "I want to go to chapel."

"No chance, Christensen. You stay in the security ward."

I acted indignant. "You are denying me freedom of religion. My attorney will sue."

"Okay, okay. The only charges we have on you is trying to commit suicide by overdosing and beating up the orderlies. If you want to go to chapel, go."

I walked with a guard down the hallway to the chapel. It was empty. "I want to meditate," I said to him.

He nodded and stayed in the hall. I closed the door, walked through the room, and out the back door. My heart revved. I did it! I ran down a couple of alleys and thumbed a ride to Corvallis.

I needed help. I needed a friend, but I couldn't go to Uncle Truman in my condition.

I went to a motel and got drunk. That was the only thing I knew to do. Maybe I could overdose again, this time for keeps, because this was it. I was at the end of the line. I had passed up the prodigal son. I was the guy with the eight demons. They would kill me, and there was nothing I could do about it.

But I couldn't overdose. The torment inside about my messed-up life got worse. It was four o'clock in the morning. I picked up the phone.

"Holly, it's Monty." I didn't let her talk. I just kept saying, "I'm so sorry. I'm sorry for everything. I want to come home. I know you hate me, but I can't take anymore. Please let me come home."

Even in my befogged mind, I heard her sleepy voice breathe, "Oh, yes, Monty, come home."

The next morning I headed back to Billings. By bus.

12

Real Christians Eat
Strawberries

Holly: Spring, 1978

"See you later." Monty closed the door and was gone.

"Monty...." She ran after him, but his car already was moving down the street.

What was going on? She went back in the house and pulled the money roll from its hiding place. Where did he get so much money? She didn't need to wonder. His actions of the past weeks meant he was back into drugs and who knew what else?

Holly pressed her stomach as if to push away the sinking feeling. Monty left her again. He wouldn't have said to get new tires if he would be around.

"Lord, what do I do?" The cry came, sounding to her ears, pathetic, miserable.

She picked up her Bible. What was it she read yesterday? It seemed to be for her. Throughout their recent problems, the Lord was teaching her to lean on

Him, to trust Him. She turned to the fifty-fifth chapter of Isaiah, and to impress words on her mind, read aloud:

> Let men cast off their wicked deeds; let them turn to the Lord that He may have mercy on them and to our God that He will abundantly pardon. This plan of mine is not what you would work out, neither are my thoughts the same as yours. For as the heavens are higher than the earth, so are my ways higher than yours and my thoughts than yours.

Holly reread the first part. It meant that God would give Monty another chance, inviting him to quit doing wicked things. It wasn't too late. She read further.

> You will live in joy and peace. The mountains and hills, the trees...all the world around you will rejoice. Where once were thorns, fir trees will grow....

Yesterday she had hope as she read that chapter. Their marriage, thorny for awhile, would again be sweet. They would have joy and peace in the house. And yet Monty left her again. What did it mean?

"Lord, You promised. I don't know how You're going to do it, but I believe You."

Jared played with his cars. "Put on your pajamas," she said. "Time for bed."

Later in her own bed, she said the promise over to

herself. It had to be true. She stretched her hand out to Monty's side. But if it were, why was his place empty.

* * *

Holly tried to balance the bulging grocery sack on one hip as she unlocked the front door.

"Telephone's ringing, Mommy," announced Jared, as he tried to help her turn the doorknob.

She dropped the sack on the coffee table and raced for the phone. Maybe it was Monty. It had been three days since he left.

"Hello?"

A man's gruff voice retorted. "I want to talk to Monty."

"He isn't here. I don't know where he is."

"Well, maybe you do and maybe you don't. He stole ten thousand from my partner and me. You tell 'em he better come up with the promised stuff or give us the money. You tell 'em." He hung up.

Holly replaced the receiver. Ten thousand. She gasped. Monty had never swindled that much money before. That's why he left. For ten thousand, they would kill him. He wouldn't come back. He left for good. She sank to a chair and cried into her cupped hands.

"Here, Mommy." Jared handed her a wadded, used tissue from his pocket. His chin quivered.

Holly hugged him fiercely. They cried together.

* * *

Jared waved good-bye at his Sunday school door, and Holly headed for the church's sanctuary.

"Holly, wait." The pastor's wife hurried toward her. "I've meant to ask you how things are going."

Holly pulled a smile to her face. "Things are fine. Monty's away."

The other woman looked into Holly's eyes as if trying to see behind them. "He left you again. Holly, he will never change. For your little boy's sake as well as your own, give up on him and lead your own life."

"Umm, well, I don't know...." Holly faltered.

"I'm sorry, Holly. I have to run. We'll pray for you, that you make the right decision." She scurried to talk to someone else.

Holly fought back tears. How could she explain the promise from the Lord? Monty was gone, but she had to hold onto it. How she wanted to ask for help. But if the pastor's wife thought Monty was a lost cause, then everyone did. They would say she misinterpreted the promise. She couldn't tell them. She'd have to try to do this by herself.

Her friend Sharon sat beside her in church. "I see we're both here by ourselves again," Sharon said. "You know, there are times I wonder if God really cares. If He did, things would be different, wouldn't they?" She nudged Holly's arm. "Shouldn't have told you that. Wish I had your strength, but sometimes...don't you ever get discouraged, Holly?"

This time Holly's smile and laugh were real. "Yes," she said, "I sure do." It helped, knowing there was one other person who didn't have all the answers.

That afternoon the telephone rang.

"You give Monty my message?" It was the man Monty swindled.

"No, I haven't seen him."

"Well, we're not waitin' any longer. We'll get our money one way or the other. You're livin' in a pretty nice trailer. It should bring us a profit for our trouble. Get your personal stuff out of it. We're pickin' it up."

"But...I don't own it. I'm just renting." It was too late. The line was dead.

* * *

Holly looked at her supervisor and swallowed hard. "My husband left me, and without a raise I can't support my son and myself," she pleaded.

"Sorry, Holly. I understand your problem, but I

145

just can't give you a raise." Holly walked out of her company's office, feeling angry, frustrated and scared. What was she to do? She called a friend from church.

"I need someone to talk to."

"Don't worry," her friend said brightly. "The Lord has another job for you. Just get out there and find it."

Her friend sounded so sure. Holly's spirits were buoyed. Now why can't I be that sure about things? Never wavering in my faith? Real Christians don't waver. "Maybe they're born that way," she laughed ruefully.

The following week she had another job and called her friend.

"See, I told you," her friend laughed. "We just have to trust."

"Yeah, I guess so," said Holly. "Just trust."

But two days into the new job, trusting again became a struggle. The former computer operator had messed up the system.

"Is there anyone who can help me understand it?" Holly asked.

"There were two people, but they were fired yesterday," said her co-worker. "And the grapevine has it that your immediate boss is being fired today."

With head pounding, Holly drove the ten miles to her country trailer. She had jumped from the proverbial skillet straight into the flames. What a mess everything was. Why had God let it get that way?

"I thought if I trusted enough, everything would be okay," Holly yelled to the ceiling, as she discovered she'd forgotten to get something for dinner. "What is it I'm not doing right? No one else has these problems!"

The doorbell rang. Holly stopped to look through the peephole. A man stood on the step, and although the screen door obscured his face, something about the way he stood reminded her of the threats. He knew she was there. She'd better open the door.

"You Monty's wife?" he asked, trying to look past her into the living room.

When she nodded, he barked, "We've given you enough time. You have to pay his debt. We're takin' the trailer."

He raised his hand to open the screen door, but Holly quickly locked it. I've got to close the door, she thought, but her legs refused to move.

"I don't own the trailer," she said, "so you can't sell it."

Legs, move out of the way.

"You ain't goin' to keep me outta here." The man shook his fist and shoved it into the screen.

All at once Holly's body obeyed her commands. She stepped back and closed the door, thumb bolting it with a snap.

"Just remember," the man shouted, "there ain't no one around here to hear ya scream."

Holly leaned against the door, taking big breaths of air. He was right. No one could hear her scream way out here. And she couldn't call the police, as someone else would do. What was she to do? Where was God?

She peeked through the curtain. The man was driving away, but when would he be back?

She ran to the bedroom where Jared played, and scooped him in her arms. "Honey," she said, her voice shaking, "we're going to the store. Mommy forgot to buy groceries. What do you want for dinner?"

They found Jared's favorites and Holly headed for the check-out. She passed the beer and wine section and looked once, then back again. Why not? She needed help sleeping tonight.

* * *

"Mommy, are we going to Sunday School? It's Sunday." Jared clambered on the bed beside Holly.

"No, Sweety, not today. It's late and Mommy has a headache. Maybe next Sunday. Can you watch cartoons for awhile?"

She watched him disappear toward the living room and closed her eyes. She and an old high school chum got together the night before—the first fun

Holly had had for a long time. She pressed her hand to her head. Trouble was, she'd forgotten how much Kathy drank, and she kept urging Holly to have one more.

Holly shook her head, still pressing her hand against the ache. She'd be in fine shape for church, wouldn't she? Her head hurt, and the pain inside was so great there were no smiles to paste on. She couldn't bear to see people whispering and giving her sidelong glances. And if they knew she spent last evening in a bar, they'd say she was a lost cause along with Monty. Maybe she was. She didn't know what she believed anymore.

One good thing, Holly thought, getting up to make breakfast for Jared, the drug people hadn't bothered her for a couple of weeks. Maybe they were all threats, but she still found herself looking behind her wherever she went.

The following Friday evening Kathy drove Holly to Jekyll's.

"This is a good idea," Holly said. "It was a terrible week. I owed myself either an evening of feeling sorry for myself, or this."

"Well, we can't have you sitting home. Besides, my brother is joining us. He's a lot of laughs." Kathy pulled into the parking lot.

It was a fun evening, Holly thought. The only thing, I wish Kathy didn't drink so much. She almost blacks out.

"Kathy," she waved her hand in front of her friend's face. "Time for me to go home."

"Sure you can drive?" Holly asked, getting in the passenger side.

"Sure, I'm sure...or whatever. Let's go. Oh, wait, my brother's truck just pulled up in back of us. Think he wants you."

Holly got out and walked back behind Kathy's bumper to talk through the door window.

Suddenly, Kathy's brother yelled, "Kathy, stop!"

Holly felt something heavy smash into the back of her knees.

The brother ran around the truck. "My God," he cried. "Holly, your left knee dented my door. We'll get you to a hospital. Kathy, how could you be so stupid?"

"Sorry," Kathy slurred. "Thought she had gone."

"I think I'm okay," Holly said, surveying her bruised knees. "I'll go home."

"The booze anesthesized you. You may have pain later," Kathy's brother warned.

At five o'clock in the morning, the pain hit. She called her mother. "Mom, this is Holly. Can you take me to the hospital?"

The emergency room doctor said, "You have a hairline fracture of your kneecap. We'll put you in a splint."

"Oh no," Holly wailed. "Then I can't drive. My car has a clutch. I'll lose my job."

For a week she stayed home, phoning computer instructions to her office.

"The boss wants to know when you're coming back, Holly. He isn't happy."

"I don't know." Holly hung up the phone and cried. "God, if I lose this job, I don't know what I'll do. Please help me."

She slammed down her computer sheets. Why should He help her? She knew what was inside her. She hated Monty for what he had done to her. Sometimes she hated her mother. She had never forgiven either of them. She had nothing but bitterness inside, and she had learned enough to know that those things put a wall between a person and God.

Yet she didn't want to give them up. In some crazy way it was comforting to hug those feelings to herself. She knew it was crazy, she knew she ought to forgive, but she didn't want to. Although she hadn't heard from Monty for six months, although she didn't know if he were dead or alive, she didn't really want to give him up either.

She didn't know what she wanted. Everything was mixed-up.

The following week, splint or no, she had to go to work or be fired. Her leg swelled to double its size and turned black-and-blue.

"That's normal," said the doctor. "It'll go away."

It did. The swelling left the upper leg and went to her ankle. Holly screamed as she saw layers of flesh drooping over her foot.

"You have phlebitis. Blood clots," pronounced the doctor. "We'll run tests."

The tests hurt worse than the blood clots. Holly cried out in pain as needles were injected all over her toes, trying to find a vein.

"You've got a huge clot in your pelvis and a bunch of them in your leg. We'll put you in the hospital on blood thinner for a few days."

The doctor didn't need to look so cheerful, Holly thought.

* * *

The days in the hospital were interminable, filled with pain, bedpans and too much thinking.

Her pastor and his wife came by to see her. "Oh, Pastor," Holly tried to wipe away the ever-present tears, "I don't know what to do about my marriage. I don't know what God is doing."

"None of us knows what to do," he responded. "Just trust Him."

"Sure," Holly said. But she thought, that's a pat answer. Everyone had pat answers to everything.

The pastor started to leave, then turned around. "Maybe, Holly, you need to really surrender to the Lord. Surrender everything. I'll be praying for you."

"Thanks," mumbled Holly. That was one answer she didn't want to hear.

When she was able to walk again, she went home with her mother for a few more days' rest. Another downer.

Sunday, her mother took Jared to church and left Holly alone. Holly was glad for the space. She did the breakfast dishes and from the corner of her eye watched the Rex Humbard program on the living room television set. What were they singing? She listened.

"Jesus, be the Lord of all the kingdoms of my heart."

Was that what was standing in the way of her peace with God? That she had never really asked Him to be Lord? That she had never given up the turmoil inside her? That she had never surrendered all the areas of her heart? Jesus had some, but others she kept for herself. Were those areas she wanted to control the reason for her roller coaster life?

Suddenly more than anything in the world, Holly wanted to give it all up. She ran to the living room and knelt at the chair by the TV. Once again, the tears flowed. And again, they were cleansing tears.

"God," she wept, "I give you all the bitterness and unforgiveness I've hung onto. I don't want it anymore. And God, I release Monty to You. It doesn't matter if he comes back or not. He's Your child, and I put him in Your hands."

As if traveling on a shaft of light, a sense of peace permeated and enveloped Holly. "Thank you Lord for forgiving me," she said in wonderment. "I've never felt like this in my entire life. You really have taken over everything. You're on the throne. And boy, am I glad."

* * *

Four days later, Holly said, "Mom, I'm going home."

Her mother protested. "Holly, you're not well enough. And I enjoy having you and Jared. Wait another week."

"No, Mom. I feel impressed to go home. Will you take me? I'd like to go to my church, too. Okay?"

Mrs. Moser smiled. "You want me to show you I'm not prejudiced against your church, is that it?"

Holly smiled back, and for the first time that she could remember, she hugged her mother.

The songs were especially good that night. Or maybe it was the change in her. The one they sang now seemed just for her. It was about praising the Lord when skies were gray, because the answer is on the way. The Lord will answer prayer.

Holly sang with her whole heart and then stopped. She heard a voice. An audible one. "You will hear from Monty tonight."

She looked around. Had anyone else heard it? It couldn't have been God talking to her. She had never had that happen before. She just wanted so much to hear from Monty, her mind played tricks. By the time she was ready for bed, she was sure of it.

The phone awakened her from a deep sleep. She looked at the clock. Four o'clock.

"Hello," she answered. In the back of her mind, she wondered if the drug people were harassing her.

"Holly, it's Monty. I'm so sorry. I want to come home."

She wasn't certain what all he said. Just the part about coming home. He loved her after all, and she answered, "Oh, yes, Monty. Oh, yes, come home."

She waited until six o'clock to awaken the pastor.

"Monty called! He's coming home!"

Next she called her friend Sharon. "Monty's coming home!"

"Great. I'll help you make a candlelight dinner and I'll watch Jared. You'll have a real reunion."

Holly floated to work. Her dreams and prayers had come true. It was a fresh beginning for them both. Days of strawberries and roses were ahead.

13

A Knight With Rusty Armor

Part 1

Holly: November, 1978

Monty was due that evening. Holly set the table with her best tablecloth and centered two candles. Sharon brought steaks and took Jared home with her. Everything would be perfect.

At six o'clock the phone rang. "Mrs. Christensen? This is the sheriff's office in Benton County, Oregon. Your husband escaped from our psychiatric clinic, and we believe he's on his way to you. Your cooperation in letting us know if he arrives would be appreciated. The longer it takes, the worse it will be for him."

Holly hung up the phone. There must be a mistake. Psychiatric clinic? Monty wasn't crazy. He would straighten it out when he came. She went back to the kitchen, singing as she put final touches on the romantic dinner.

Every so often she looked at the clock. He should

be here by now. Maybe he had an accident. "No, God, I'm not taking back the worry. You're on the throne." Still, it was after ten.

Car lights shone in the window, waking her. The clock chimed midnight. Dripping wax from the burned-down candles mounded on the tablecloth. The door bell rang, and her heart leaped. This wasn't the way she'd planned, but he was home. She uncurled herself from her chair and smoothed her hair.

"Welcome home!" she said, opening the door. Then she clamped her hand over her mouth.

It was Monty. Hair to his shoulders, grubby jeans and jacket. He swayed unsteadily.

The cab driver stood behind him. "You going to pay his fare?"

"Yes, of course." Holly ran for her purse. "God, what are You doing?"

* * *

Monty fell asleep on the couch and was still asleep when Holly left for work the next morning. That evening, she came home, Jared in tow.

"Where's my daddy?" Jared raced through the house.

Monty was gone.

"Honey, he'll be back after awhile. I know he'll want to see some of your drawings."

"I'll make him some new ones." Jared trotted to his room.

The telephone rang. "Mrs. Christensen, this is the Oregon sheriff's department again. Has your husband made contact?"

"No," Holly said. "No, he hasn't." Lord, please forgive that lie.

"Well, let us know. He's wanted by the state of Montana for parole violation."

Dinner time came and went. Still no Monty.

"I guess he had things to do," she consoled Jared as she got him ready for bed. "You'll see him tomorrow."

Close to midnight Holly dropped to her knees. "Lord, he didn't come home for me. He doesn't want me. I made the mistake. You didn't. I still give him to You."

She went to bed to dream of princesses and handsome knights driving white Mustangs.

The next afternoon when she got home from work, Monty was there. "Wanted to play with my son," he said, swooping Jared on his shoulders.

"Monty, the Oregon sheriff called twice."

"You tell him I was here?"

"No, but you've got to give yourself up and straighten this out."

"I will. After Christmas. We want to have a nice Christmas, don't we? By the way, do you have any money?"

"Only a little for Christmas shopping."

"Well, I really need it tonight. I'll repay it in a couple of days, and we'll both go shopping."

Holly gave him a fifty-dollar bill. She had a sinking feeling she wouldn't see it again. Then without even a kiss, he was out the door.

Why did I give him the money? She slammed her purse on the table. "God, nothing's changed. What happened to Your promise? How much more testing do I need to prove I meant it when I gave him to You?"

* * *

Holly let herself in the house the following day. Monty was on the telephone, his back to her.

"I'll work it out. Don't worry." His voice dropped when he saw Holly, and he quickly hung up. "Just talking to some of the guys," he said. "Say, I need some money. Can you find some while I shower and shave?"

This time I won't give him much, Holly thought, emptying her change purse. A coin dropped and rolled under the bed, and she felt around for it. There was something else under there. She pulled out a woman's picture and a letter addressed to Monty at their address.

"Monty, who is this?"

Monty barely looked at them. "Oh, that's a gal I met. She has a thing for a friend here in Billings. Wanted me to give him her picture, but didn't have his address. I'll take it." He put the letter and picture in his pocket.

Holly didn't say anything. She did wonder why Monty had thrown them under the bed.

After he was gone, the pastor stopped by with an envelope. "Holly, someone at church didn't know why they were to do it, but felt impressed to leave you this for your Christmas shopping."

Inside was a fifty dollar bill.

"Lord," Holly said, looking upward, "I'm not sure I remembered to specifically release my money to You, but guess You understood I did. Thanks." She would shop tomorrow evening. It would be a good Christmas.

But everyone in the office felt the Christmas rush, and Holly was extra tired the next evening. An early bedtime would be nice. Monty was getting ready for his nightly round of bars as she climbed under the covers.

She didn't fall asleep. She thought about Christmas presents. Maybe Monty would like to shop with her. She padded into the living room and heard Monty's voice.

"I miss you, too. Yes, I want to get married. There are things I have to straighten out. Uh, Marcy, I'm married. Should have told you sooner. I'm working on a divorce...." He turned and saw Holly. "Umm, I've got to hang up now."

With each word, a separate shock wave hit Holly. She stood numb, nauseous tentacles spreading throughout her body.

"Holly...."

But Holly turned and walked back to bed, pulling the covers over her head. She heard the door slam and burst into sobs. "This isn't fair. I trusted You, God. I released him. I prayed. I did all the things You wanted me to do. And all the time he was with her. Now I've lost him, and You don't seem to care." Thoughts of Monty and the girl whirled through Holly's mind, and her sobs grew harder, until at last she fell into an exhausted sleep.

Sunday in church, Sharon hugged her. "How's it going?"

"Not great," Holly confessed. "Monty was still in bed when I left. He acts as if he never knew there was a God. And there are other things. It's tough to hold on."

Holly thought more about Monty than the sermon that morning. It was half over when she snapped to attention. Was the pastor talking straight to her?

"When we first approached God, every one of us was grubby and dirty and smelly," he said. "And we weren't there to immediately love Him and have a great relationship with Him. We came to Him because we needed help. We would die if we didn't come to Him."

Holly sat straighter. That was Monty. He didn't come home to her because of his love. He needed her help. So...she inwardly urged the pastor...what did God do?

As if answering her question, the pastor said, "God knew all that, but He accepted us the way we were—no changing. Then He loved us with the kind of love that's irresistible. He demonstrated His patience, kindness, faithfulness—and His joy. Do you think that's impossible for you to do with those around you?"

Yes. Holly nearly said it aloud. *Yes.*

"If you think it is, here are three steps to prove it isn't."

I don't believe this, Holly said to herself. Well, what are the steps? She snatched a pen from her purse and scribbled on the church's morning bulletin.

"Number one," the pastor said, "you yourself need to be a born-again Christian. You can't do anything without that. When you have God's Spirit in you, He can demonstrate love and patience and kindness."

"Second, pray and praise. Pray that the Lord will strengthen you in those fruits of His Spirit, and then praise and thank Him for doing it."

"Third, go for it, even if it's hard. Practice love. Practice kindness. And keep it up."

After the service, Holly went to the altar to pray and settle things in her mind. "Lord, I'm your child, and You have placed Your Spirit in me. Please strengthen me in Your special kind of love. Give me a real love for Monty. Help me accept him just as he is, and I praise and thank You for doing it. Amen."

She left with a peaceful heart, realizing this project might take days—weeks.

That evening, sitting on the couch beside Monty, she picked up the phone when it rang. A woman's voice asked, "Is Monty there?"

Holly handed the phone to Monty and continued to sit beside him.

"Oh, hi, Marcy. Yeah, that was my wife. Well, you know the situation. Sure. I'd like to see you...."

A knife twisted in Holly's heart. The pain was worse than the phlebitis tests. Worse than any pain she had ever had. Why was he torturing her? Maybe she should turn him in. It was after Christmas, after the time he promised he would surrender. It would serve him right. And it would keep this other woman away from him.

Suddenly in the back of her mind came the words, "I thought you decided to go for it."

It was the Holy Spirit's prompting, she knew that.

"Yes, Lord," she said inwardly, "I will. Thank You for Your love."

She took Monty's free hand in hers and squeezed it. Like a sudden rainshower, she was at once engulfed in compassion for him. Along with the compassion, came a love like she had never had. The kind that brought with it acceptance— for how he was and what he was doing. No matter if it hurt. She sat quietly as he talked. Pray and praise and practice. She would stay out on that limb.

* * *

The pork roast and browned potatoes sent their aroma through the house. It was a month after Christmas, and Holly was practicing her fruits of the Spirit by cooking a nice dinner. Monty was in the shower. After dinner he would leave for his rendez- vous with the bars. She knew it, but forced herself to hum as she set three plates on the table opposite the front door.

At the bell's summons, she opened the door wide. Four policemen stared back at her. Their glances took in everything in the living room and settled on the dining table set with three place settings.

"Is Monty Christensen here?" one of them asked.

At first Holly couldn't move or speak. What should she do? Someone had pushed the off button on her brain. She found her voice. "Just a minute, please." She turned to go. Close the door, she said to herself and slammed it in their faces. "I'll be right back," she yelled.

She ran to the bathroom and pounded on the door. "Monty, Monty, the police are here asking for you. What should I tell them?"

"Well, for Pete's sakes, tell them I'm not here!"

"Oh, okay," she said, and ran back, but the police had surrounded the trailer, one of them listening at the bathroom side.

"Ma'am," said one of the officers. "We know he's in there. Shall we wait until he comes out, or do you want to let us in?"

Holly felt like a balloon stretched to its max, having a pin stuck in it. Suddenly she was tired. Tired of always being in the middle of everything. "Come in, Officer. He's getting dressed."

"Guess this is it," Monty said, hugging Holly and Jared.

The police handcuffed him.

"What are they doing to Daddy?" cried Jared, pulling at the officer's pant leg to make him stop.

With streaming tears, Holly and Jared watched the police cars pull away. It was nearly midnight, but Holly called Sharon. "I need to talk to someone. Would you come over?"

"You know," said Sharon, after the two cried together, "this may be an opportune time for God to work. Hebrews 1:14 says He sends angels to minister to those who are to receive salvation. Let's pray that He dispatches a bunch of them to start things moving—to intercept wrong passes and put key people in key places. Come on, Girl—get ready for battle."

Part Two

Monty: January, 1979

I didn't look back. I couldn't stand seeing Jared, frightened and crying.

In the police car I leaned my head on the back of the car seat. Here we go again. I didn't want to surrender. Who wants to go to jail? But in a strange way it was a relief to have the uncertainty over with. And a relief to get away from Holly.

She had told me she accepted me the way I was. And she loved me. Nothing could change it. She was so sweet and kind to me, no matter how I treated her. I couldn't handle it. It made me feel like a heel and I didn't want to feel anything.

So I was out from under that, plus all her praying friends. I didn't want anyone praying for me. Changing my life. It wouldn't be as easy for them now.

At the jail, it was the same old thing. They stripped me and gave me a pair of coveralls with YELLOWSTONE COUNTY JAIL on the back.

"Want to make a phone call before we take you to your cell?"

"Yeah," I said, "to Oregon." I'd call Marcy. Let her know where she could write me. Maybe visit.

I dialed the operator. "This is Monty Christensen, and I want to make...."

"Monty!" said the operator. "How nice. This is Barbara from the Park Hill Church. I want you to know that I love you and I'm praying for you. Now, who did you want to call?"

"I...I've changed my mind." Out of sixty thousand people in town and more than five hundred working for the telephone company, how did she happen to be my operator?

* * *

Cells, bullpens, too many men. The usual stuff. I stretched out on a floor mattress. Coming down from speed, coke and whiskey wouldn't be fun. Already my stomach contracted. It needed a fix.

It got worse. Three days of vomiting, and a flaming knot in my guts.

Toward the end of the period, the guard shook me. "Got a visitor. Five minutes."

I stumbled to the visiting room and looked through the window of the steel door. It was Holly— smiling her sweet smile. Incredible.

"Get away from me, and stay away from me!" I

yelled at her. "I don't want anything to do with you or your love. In a few days they're transferring me to prison—away from you. And in order to survive, I'll be the meanest, the most hateful, most violent guy there. Just watch. Then see how much you love me. Good-bye!" I stormed back to my cell and threw up.

The next day a guy from the outside spoke in chapel. It was a chance to get out of my cell. I sat there, tuning him out, thinking about Marcy and other things. Afterward he came up to me and shook hands. "I'm Ken Mitchell. Glad to meet you."

We sat and talked for awhile. I had ready answers in case he zeroed in on me to "get right with God." But he didn't talk Bible at all. As he rose to leave, he said, "Monty, you're a neat person. I'd like to spend time getting to know you. See you the next time I come?"

I said, "I'll be out of here in another week, but okay, I'll see you before I leave." I hadn't intended to say that, but he took me by surprise. Imagine someone just wanting to spend time with me.

Holly came again with a stack of books and my favorite chocolate cookies. I only saw her because I wanted to tell her again that we were through.

But my words didn't daunt her. "Monty, I love you, and I won't give up. I have fourteen prayer warriors praying for you—about prison, everything." She laughed. "They're doing battle in the heavenlies, and something good will come from it. And by the way, Pastor Bob from church will be here to see you."

"Oh, yeah," I answered. "Well, I'm leaving here in

a few days, so guess I'll have to forego the honor of meeting him. You and your prayer warriors have struck out."

I left and went back to my cell. Prison couldn't come too soon for me. At least there would be more things to do, and I wouldn't have to see anyone just for the privilege of getting out of my cell. I picked up one of Holly's books. Religious. I threw it down. And no more of them.

"Christensen," the sheriff's deputy looked in at me. "Just got word. The state prison employees went on strike. With less crew, they can't handle more prisoners. You'd better plan on being here for awhile."

14

Steadfast Love

Part One

Holly: February, 1979

"Want to try the new restaurant for lunch, Holly?"

"Can't." Holly looked up from the office computer.

"Today's visiting day at jail. I'll take a later lunch hour, so I can drive up to see Monty."

"You really go out of your way for him. Frankly I don't think men are worth it." The co-worker shook her head as she went out the door.

Holly smiled, then laughed as she thought, "Wonder if God ever thought that about all of us? 'Thanks Jesus, for going out of Your way for me.'"

Shortly after two o'clock she pulled into the jail parking lot and bowed her head. "Lord, I wish I weren't here. You know how hard these visits are.

Please fill me with Your love and patience. I thank and praise You for the miracle You are performing, even if I don't see it yet."

She grabbed the magazines and snacks she brought and walked into the jail. Would Monty come to the visiting room?

He did, but all she saw in his face and eyes was hardness. Indifference.

"Thanks for the cookies," he said. "How's Jared?"

"Fine. Maybe he'll come Sunday." Holly swallowed hard. "Monty...Marcy called me. She said she would come to see you." She hadn't wanted to tell him. She fought the tears.

Monty nodded. "She wrote me that. Well, gotta go."

"Monty, I love you." Holly put her hand to the window, but Monty turned and walked away.

The drive back to the office was difficult. Tears blurred her vision.

That evening, opening her mail, her heart almost stopped. The telephone bill was nearly one hundred fifty dollars. Monty's long distance calls. How would she ever pay that? She had the medical bills from her phlebitis and still no settlement from the insurance company. The tears flowed again. "Lord, I'm behind on my car payment and now this. I feel like I'm sinking. I'm going under. Where are You?"

From the inner corridors of her mind, a gentle

voice came, "You surrendered everything to Me—yourself, Monty. Do you think these bills are too hard for Me? Surrender them."

Holly wiped her eyes. "All right. They're Your bills now, and I guess You've got the money. What I can do is send in fifty dollars, so the phone company knows I'm honest."

She blew her nose. This surrendering business wasn't a breeze. It had to be done every day.

Part Two

Monty:

A prison strike. I slammed my fist into the mattress. Why did it have to happen now? Maybe it wouldn't last long. I could still be out of here in a couple of days.

My spirits lifted at that thought, so when the guard announced that a Pastor Bob waited in the library, I went. It was something to do, and it was a special feeling to be called out. Someone cared about you. The guys who never had visitors always looked envious.

The pastor was about my age. He pumped my hand. "Hi, Monty. Heard a lot about you. There are a lot of people praying you'll get back to God."

Whoa. This guy came on strong. Still there was an eagerness about him that I liked. Did he remind me of myself? Through all his overzealousness, he really liked me. So instead of going back to the dingy cell, I let him talk, throwing in a few statements or questions I knew would stump him.

"The Bible is contradictory," I said, feeling smug. "It says God forgives over and over, but it also says He's a just God. If He's just, He can't keep forgiving. He has to draw the line someplace."

"No, Monty, the Bible isn't contradictory. In this instance, you have to know more about God. He isn't like us humans. We may forgive, but it's difficult for us to forget. When God forgives, He has the divine ability to forget. He's forgotten the last time you asked for forgiveness. He's forgotten your past sins. That's why His forgiveness can be never-ending."

"Then He's a patsy," I said. I didn't look at Bob.

"No way. He just has that much love for you. I have to go. See you next week."

"I'll be out of here by then," I said.

I went back to my cell and got out a sheet of paper. I'd write Marcy. She could visit me in prison.

My glance fell on a marriage book Holly brought. Some couple getting back together. "She never gives up," I said aloud. "After everything, why doesn't she give up?"

I heard the zealous minister's voice, "God's forgiveness is never-ending. He just has that much love for you."

God and Holly, I thought. They both go beyond

seventy times seven. I threw down the sheet of paper. Maybe I'd write Marcy tomorrow.

* * *

The strike continued. I had been in jail four weeks. Men waiting for transfer to the prison stacked up in the cells like cord wood.

I reached out in the middle of the confusion to touch Ken's and Bob's stability, their caring. I looked forward to their visits. And whether I liked it or not, Holly's visits were becoming important.

One visiting day it came to me with a jolt that what I was seeing through the screened window was my wife. *My* wife. Pretty, faithful, caring of my needs. She was mine. The thought overwhelmed me. She looked tired. Maybe she was—sick and tired of going out of her way, just to receive the responses I gave her.

"Will you come again?" I asked.

She looked startled, as if that were the last thing she expected to hear me ask. She laughed, her voice sounding within the cold, stark room, like a beloved melody. "Of course I will, Monty. I love you. And I'll always be here."

She put her hand to the window, and for the first time, I placed my hand opposite hers. I felt funny inside. A familiar, good kind of funny.

I went back to my cell and buried my head in my

hands. "Oh, God, I'm sorry for the way I've treated Holly and Jared. Forgive me, please."

This time there was no big explosion in my life. As the days in jail stretched, God softened my scabbed-over heart. I could feel a difference. I eased back to Him slowly, but certainly. The relationship I had had with Him, every experience we had ever shared, now seemed to be bedrock, giving me sure footing. It was as if there had never been a gap. I also committed myself to the fact that I was married to Holly and that we would work things out.

After Sunday visiting times, Holly and Jared and the Afghans we gave each other the year before, stood on the street corner across from the jail. Holly and Jared waved. I grabbed a towel and flagged it through the bars. "Hey, look," I told the guys around me. "See down there? That's *my* wife. That's *my* boy. Those are *our* dogs."

* * *

How can a person be happy in jail? But I was. I was at peace with God and Holly. While I didn't relish the thought of going to prison, it wasn't as frightening as before.

Only one thing bothered me. Now that I was back with the Lord, I wanted to serve Him, to minister as I had before, but nothing seemed to be happening. I shared this with Pastor Bob.

"It's almost as if a barrier stood in the way," I said.

Bob looked at me thoughtfully. "Monty, have you cleaned up your whole act? I mean, are there any loose ends from your former life that need to be attended to?"

I didn't have to search my mind. I knew what it was, or rather, who. Marcy. In my innate cowardice, I hadn't told her of my newfound commitment. If I didn't think about her, she'd go away. But God was telling me it didn't work that way.

I wrote to her that afternoon, telling her that it was over between us. I wouldn't divorce my wife. I had to make things right with her and with my marriage. I struggled over each word, but when the letter was on its way, a wonderful sense of release flooded through me. There were no more dangling strings.

That night one of the guys in my cell said, "Monty, I've been watching you. I've got a lot of years waitin' for me in prison, and I can't handle it. It doesn't bother you. How come?"

My first real opportunity to share Christ. Well, God, guess You think I'm ready to work. Here we go.

The guy accepted Christ into his heart and the next morning said, "Hey, this is the first time in my life I woke up feelin' good. Everything's cool."

I was about to give him words of wisdom, when the guard pushed another prisoner into the cell. I did a double take. It was Charley, my former drug-fronter.

He looked at me in horror. "Hey, Man, I've been trying to stay outta your way. I'm really sorry I ripped you off that time. Everybody in town told me you were out gunning for me—threatened to blow off their kneecaps if they didn't squeal. But I have to tell ya—I accepted Christ a few months ago. I'm changed."

I laughed and put out my hand. "Well, Charley, meet another guy who's been given the chance to begin life all over again. I'm born-again, and I forgive you." I shook my head. "Isn't this something? I would have killed you back then. Now we are brothers in Christ. We can be friends."

Things were popping. For the next few days, men would be temporarily assigned to my cell, accept Christ, and leave. I started a Bible study, and the prisoners came running. We sang the roof off.

"With all these guys in here, it's peaceful. I don't understand it," said the head guard.

However one disappointment was the guy in the cell next to mine. He was in for stealing mag wheels. One night as I lay on my mattress, I mentally laid hands on him and prayed. A strong inner witness said, "Monty, he won't come to Me. There's something he won't admit about himself, so he can't receive Me."

This is ridiculous, I thought. That's either the devil or me talking, and I kept praying for the guy. The same inner voice said, "He will not confess; therefore, he can't come to Me."

I gave up. "Okay, Lord," I said quietly. "What do you mean?"

The voice said, "This man committed incest, but won't admit it. He can't receive Me even if you pray."

"Okay," I said and mentally took my hands off him.

The next morning I talked to him about his heart and about Jesus the way I did to the other guys. When I did that, even murderers would pray with me, but not this one. He didn't want to talk about anything spiritual.

The next week, the word was out. The guy had charges of incest on him. "They're lying," he said. He left the jail, not admitting who he was and not accepting Christ.

Sometimes I had to pour out my feelings to Holly in letters.

> Holly, I feel special tonight because when I get down or start to feel depressed, I can read the Bible and praise God and pray with thanks, and *wow*, I'm back in the swing, unless the Lord is trying to deal with me about something specific. Then because of my usual foolish pity-party, it takes a little more waiting on Him.
>
> Sometimes at night in my mind, I lay my hands on each guy here and pray. I believe it is this that brings many of them to me when they're down about something, a common

occurrence around this depressing place. All
I can do is share Christ, pray for them, and
encourage them to come to our Bible study.
The rest is definitely up to them.

The prison strike is over, and one by one
men are leaving. I'll see them when I get
there, probably next week. Give a hug to
Jared.

Love always, Monty

I still was apprehensive about Holly's feelings for
me. It was a long, hard haul, and she was outside,
surrounded by guys out for a good time. So I eagerly
tore open her next letter.

Dear Monty,

I'm glad you have a Christian inmate with
you because fellowship with other Christians
strengthens us. Boy, are the rest of the guys
in for it.

I sure miss you. If you go to the Deer Lodge
prison, I'll make arrangements to be there
next week end. Please be secure knowing I
never went the ways of the wicked in the
world and that I'll never turn back from you or
God. I want to mature in Jesus, and I want
His love and light to shine through me.

God is so good. He brought us together, this
time for good. With Him, all things are possible. I praise Him for even the circumstances
we are in because each of us will draw closer
to Him through these afflictions. God is pre-

paring us for a ministry that will bring Him glory. We have so much ahead of us. Monty, this poem is how I feel.

"I am married, and my heart is glad;

I will give thanks unto the Lord for the love and protection of my husband.

I will give thanks for the satisfaction of my home;

I will give thanks that I have someone of my own to help and comfort and even worry about,

My husband is beside me wherever I need to go,

My husband is behind me, supporting me in whatever I need to do.

I need not face the world alone,

I need not face my family alone,

I need only to face myself and my God alone and this is good.

Whatever our differences, whatever our trials, I will give thanks to the Lord for my husband and my marriage,

For as long as I have both my husband and my God,

I am a woman complete; I am not alone."

I love you, Monty.

I held the letter close to me and cried. God indeed was good.

Part Three

Holly:

Holly pulled the cupcakes from the oven and got the powdered sugar to make Jared's favorite frosting. It was a special treat. He was a wonderful little boy, preferring to go see his daddy on Sunday afternoons instead of playing with his friends. During the long waiting time, he colored or worked on his Sunday school paper. How she thanked God each day that He gave them a boy like Jared.

She swirled on the icing. As long as she had Monty and Jared, all other problems were minimal. A long sigh escaped. Even the financial problems. Before she sent the fifty dollars to the telephone company, the company notified her that they would disconnect her phone. The bank sent notice that the car would be repossessed if she didn't make a payment. That meant she couldn't get to work or to Deer Lodge to see Monty. But she had determined weeks ago that she wouldn't ask her mom for a loan. She surrendered it to God, and it was up to Him.

It was Saturday, and the mail was late. The usual pile of bills, one from the phone company. A knot grew in Holly's stomach. It would be their final warning about her service. I won't open it, she thought, but she resolutely ripped the seal. "Thank you for your complete payment." What? Holly looked again. The amount paid was one hundred fifty dollars. What happened? She riffled through the mail for the bank statement. There was her check, the one for fifty dollars. Except on the bottom, in code, it said one hundred fifty.

Holly fell into a chair, laughing and crying. She would pay it back, of course, but the entire system messed up just so she could have her telephone. She waved the check to the ceiling. "Lord, You have a sense of humor."

After the Sunday church service, the pastor beckoned Holly aside. "Holly, the church family wants to show you and Monty that we love you both and support you. We know about your car problem...and...well, here's a check to pay your monthly car payment. Hope it helps."

This time Holly's tears flowed without laughter. They fell on the feet of Jesus, and through Him onto the pastor.

* * *

This is the last time I'll be coming here, Holly thought, looking around the waiting room. Jared sat quietly, working on his spelling words for school. They were waiting for permission to go to Monty's floor. Another woman sat in the chair opposite them.

She had been coming almost as long as Holly, and while they never exchanged more than a few words, they always smiled at each other. Holly noticed that the woman watched her out of the corner of her eye.

This time the woman said, "We've been comin' here a long time. My name's Emily. My man Lamar is leavin' tomorrow for the penitentiary."

"Oh," said Holly. "Mine's leaving soon, too." Inwardly she thought, "How am I going to stand it? He'll be so far away, and it will be so long. Now come on, Holly," she chided herself. "You can't let Monty see you depressed."

She tried to smile and talk of cheerful things when she saw him. "Monty, a gal I've seen here a lot says her husband is leaving tomorrow. His name's Lamar. Do you know him?"

"Sure do. I led him to the Lord recently. He's a good man. Maybe I'll get a chance to see him up there. Lamar will be a solid Christian, and he really loves his wife. Talks about her a lot."

There was an awkward pause. Neither of us know what to say or do, Holly thought. Suddenly her faith and good intentions broke down. She couldn't handle it. "Monty, what's going to happen to you in that awful prison? What's going to happen to us? To our future? Seventy years. Oh, Monty." She started to cry.

Monty looked forlorn. "I don't know," he said. "We just have to trust God."

184

"Well, sometimes I need more than that." Dabbing a tissue to her eyes, Holly left.

The next day, Holly spent her lunch hour walking. "Lord," she said, "I'm sorry I lost it yesterday. You've proven Yourself in the past, and I know You won't leave us dangling. I trust You with whatever is in our future. You won't let anything hurt us." She stuffed her hands deep in her pockets and tried to ignore the stares of a little boy, fascinated by a lady mouthing words with no sound. "But Lord, I'm worried about Monty—what I did to him yesterday. I must have discouraged him so much. I may have undone everything we've accomplished. Could you fix it please?"

That evening, the mail brought a letter from Monty. So soon? Holly wondered. She opened it, a lump of fear rising in her throat.

Dear Holly,

After you left, I sat down to write this. First of all, I want to say how good God is in keeping me here in jail. I had time to fall in love with you again, and we've had time to begin a new relationship.

I don't mean to be alien to our problems by hiding behind God, but I have no other answer for the things we face, except from the Word of God. Faith, endurance, long-suffering, and patience. We get a chance to practice them. Would you mind praying with me? Pretend we're together.

Father, You know the pain and suffering that Holly and I face every day in being anxious for each other. How we long to be together and get on with all that You've taught us. And to begin building a relationship in You.

Lord, hear our prayers, and honor our faith as we believe You for the miracle of a soon reunion. We desire Your will so we don't fall into having troubled spirits. So please, Lord, give us both patience, long-suffering and endurance. Daily build our faith in You.

Tonight, comfort Holly and me in all Your decisions for our lives as we wait, believing for Your best for us. Thank You, Father, for hearing and answering our prayers. In Jesus Christ's name we pray. Amen.

Goodnight, Holly. Sleep tight.

15

Prison-Yard Orchard

Monty:

After being kept on ice for seven weeks, suddenly I was at the airport on my way to the Deer Lodge Penitentiary. I had been through the indoctrination procedure before, but it was never routine. It never lost its humiliation.

"Here's your number. Strip." barked a guard. The other prisoners and I obeyed, and while we stood shivering in front of a platoon of guards, they cut our hair and shaved us. They sprayed us for lice and took our pictures.

"Come on, Man, not like this. Not naked," protested a young prisoner.

"Shut up. You speak when you're spoken to."

They watched as we put on prison clothes. One burly guard singled me out. "You came in here with some sort of Bible. That won't get you out." Before I could respond, he grabbed the front of my shirt. "To me, you're less than a piece of sh—." He laughed. "I'm going to do everything I can to step on you."

I felt the back of my neck grow hot. Why was he saying that? I hadn't done anything to him. My mind flashed me back to being six years old. Slapped, humiliated. I wanted to smash this guy's face as I smashed my old Tonka toys. Silently I yelled for help. "Lord, I prayed for long-suffering. Thank You for giving me Yours right now."

My parole officer gave me the word. With all the states' charges, I had a total of seventy-five or more years rolled up. When I finished my minimum ten-year sentence in Montana, I would go to Oregon for forty more. Then to Idaho and New Mexico. That is, if I were still alive. And they planned on making all the charges stick. He said the last in obvious glee.

I was put in close custody. No chance for escape. And there was a mandatory two-week blackout. I couldn't communicate with anyone. Except God.

My Bible disappeared. I asked the chaplain if he had one I could use.

He smiled a bland kind of smile. "No, sorry, I don't have Bibles to hand out to people. Sometimes people want them out of guilt. Can't you wait until your blackout is over and ask a family member for one?"

"No," I said. "I really need one."

With a patronizing look, he said, "All right, I'll see what I can do." The next week he brought one to me. "Got to try to pull yourself up, Christensen. You can do anything you determine to do."

"Ever tried to get off drugs?" I asked.

He didn't answer.

Two weeks of blackout did its job discouraging me. When I finally got to write Holly, my letters weren't uplifting.

Sweetheart,

Here I sit in the worst part of the prison, what they call "behind the walls." This place is ancient. I'm in a small cell, six feet by nine, seven feet high. Twelve-inch concrete walls with a small door of bars at one end.

This is the oldest of all state prisons. A decrepit mess. From what I can see, it's a huge building with four levels, one on top of each other with a catwalk around each tier. Outside is a high rock wall.

I'm in a daze because they showed me signed papers from Oregon saying I go there from here. This mess is hard to understand, but I'm not confused or bitter. I'm at peace, knowing God is working all things out. Praise His name for His comfort in trials. I hope and pray the same for you. My love, I know this will be a nightmare for you. Please know I love you very much.

Before the ink dried on that letter, I dashed off another. Just writing the letter made me feel close to Holly.

—Here I am in hell on earth, but am not crushed. You wouldn't believe this run-down hole. Windows in the cell houses are broken out, and snow comes in. We never seem to be warm. It's always cold.

Slimy silverfish are all over—in our clothes, our beds, and I wouldn't doubt, in our food. Although they spray for lice, those crawly things are all over the place, too. But mainly it's cold.

I was marched into a different building for chow. This will be the extent of my outings for awhile. As I walked along, on the wall were two guards with rifles resting on their hips. A deadly sight, an Ar-15 always looking down on you.

I trust that you will also praise the Lord for our trials, for I love you and may be gone a long time. I trust you completely, Holly, and will always love and cherish you as my wife.

Monty

"Time for chapel," came the announcement.

"Great," I said. I grabbed my Bible and marched along the catwalk.

Other men meandered out of their cells. No Bibles in sight. "Going to chapel?" I asked a couple of them.

"Uh...not sure...we'll see," said one, nervously.

"Me? Oh, no...just going to the library," said another, too loudly, I thought.

They were in chapel, giving me half-embarrassed looks, along with others, pulling tiny Bibles from pockets or larger ones from hiding.

What was going on? These men must be Christians, yet too intimidated to stand up for what they believed in. How could other prisoners be won to Christ?

As I pondered, the Holy Spirit suddenly gave me a larger burden for souls than I had ever had. Inside I wept for the men in the prison. Men who were in the continual pattern of going back and tasting the vomit of their former sins—their former life-style. Men, who like me, let Satan destroy them.

But alongside the tears, like another lane on a freeway, came a stream of hope. God and two others made a three-fold cord that wasn't easily broken. If two of us agreed as touching anything, we could make ten thousand flee. Well, there were only seven hundred fifty men in that prison. And even with all the demons involved with them, two of us and God could see the penitentiary won to Jesus.

The thought kept me elated the rest of the day, but later when I read the thirty-fourth chapter of Ezekiel for my daily Bible reading, I almost went through the roof. The twenty-seventh verse pulsated with confirmation of what the Lord said earlier: "When I have broken off their chains of slavery and delivered them from those who profiteered at their expense, they shall know I am the Lord."

As if the Lord wanted me to know He really meant it, a letter arrived the following day from Holly.

Dear Monty,

I am so glad the blackout is over. Those two weeks were long. I've missed you so much and look forward to next weekend when I can drive up to see you. I've arranged to take every other Friday off work so we can have a long weekend every two weeks.

The conditions there sound awful. I'll pray they don't overwhelm you.

I have an attorney working on the charges. Guess we both have to lean harder on the Lord, which is maybe why we're going through all this. Some people have crossroads or options to trust the Lord or lean on their own doing. We have to trust Him, so guess we'll learn the lesson more quickly than some others.

Even if it looks impossible, I know the Lord will use you in a mighty way to minister to those men. Last night I picked up the Living Bible for my daily reading, and one verse especially stood out as if it were for your situation:

When I have broken off their chains of slavery and delivered them from those who profiteered at their expense, they shall know I am the Lord. (Ezek. 34:27)

Monty, I feel that's what the Lord will do through you to the prisoners there. I'll stand by you in prayer. I love you. Jared loves you and sends a kiss and this latest drawing. See you soon.

Holly

I raised my hands over my head and gave the Lord a round of applause. For the mighty thing He was promising He would do, for the individual growth in both Holly and me—and for making us a team that together with Him couldn't be beaten. No matter what happened.

16

Two Kisses Allowed

Holly:

Holly pulled up her coat collar and shivered as she left her mother's house. The sun hadn't risen high enough to soften the bitterness of this March morning.

Jared was disappointed that he couldn't see his dad, but this first prison visit, it was better he stayed with Mom. Holly didn't know what she was getting into, what to expect.

In a few minutes she left Billings behind. "Here we go, God," she said. "Only four hours and forty-five minutes more to see Monty." As her tire studs bit into the snow crust, she hummed a few praise choruses, then sang at the top of her voice.

How grateful she was that the insurance settlement came in time. Without it, she couldn't afford the gas to drive to Deer Lodge, much less the lodging.

She got into Deer Lodge an hour before the visiting time and drove around town looking for a motel. When she found one, she unloaded her bags and asked the clerk for directions to the prison.

The woman looked Holly up and down. Her eyebrows raised. "I wouldn't have taken you for a wife."

Holly laughed. "But I am a wife. I'm married." She had a strong feeling that she was being judged and condemned in one glance.

"Oh, I mean a wife of one of...those." The clerk bobbed her head toward the prison. "I can usually pick 'em out. Hard-looking, come in by bus or with somebody. On welfare, skip out without payin'."

"Oh, I don't think all wives are like that," protested Holly.

"Hmmph," responded the woman.

That can't be what the whole town thinks of inmates and their wives, thought Holly as she drove into the penitentiary's parking lot. It's so unfair.

She looked up at the building. Monty's descriptions were accurate. It was a monstrosity, like an evil castle.

A line had already formed outside a door in the rock wall.

"Are you waiting to go in?" she asked another woman.

"Sure, Honey. Hurry up and wait. Hurry up and wait. They make 'em do it inside, and make us do it out here. First time, huh? You'll learn."

Holly rubbed her hands together and moved her legs back and forth to keep warm. She looked at the other women. Many did have hard faces. Hurt too many times, Holly thought. Most wore a lot more makeup than Holly did, and nearly all of them eyed Holly's clothes and the bag of goodies she brought for Monty.

She was relieved when the door was unlocked. The line walked through the prison yard and up to the main building. Holly caught her breath. In a wire cage, a guard watched them, his hand close to his gun. The reality of where she was hit. Monty had to endure this every hour of every day. For how many more years? She bit her lip hard to keep from crying.

In the visiting room there was a sudden rush toward the wooden tables, and occasional bickering over who got to the small ones first.

"See, Honey," said the woman she had talked to outside. "The trick is, get in line first so you and your man get a single table. Makes it nicer."

Well, guess she's right, Holly said to herself. I'll learn. She sat down at the end of a long table where two families already talked and laughed. She waited.

Then Monty was there. Really Monty. Tall and handsome. How wonderful to touch him. He kissed her slow and hard. "It's good to be home," he whispered.

Holly didn't say anything, but started to kiss him

again when the guard intervened.

"Only two kisses allowed. One before the visit and one after."

"Oh," said Holly. Still, they could hold hands. They sat down.

"Monty, I've decided this commuting back and forth for who knows how long is ridiculous. Jared and I will move to Deer Lodge, and I'll get a job here."

"No, Sweetheart. I don't want you mixed up in the kind of things going on in the prison community. You'd be approached to smuggle drugs and if you didn't...."

"Drugs!" Holly clamped her hand over her mouth. "Are drugs smuggled into prison?" she whispered.

Monty looked around to see if anyone heard. "And you and Jared would be ostracized. There's a black cloud over all prison towns. I've seen it. Although the prison supports the town, the town looks at us as the whole cause of society's problems. An inmate's family is immediately condemned. I know the trip's a hassle, and I worry about you, but it's better. In fact, bring the dogs next time if you can. Now what did you bring me? Chocolate cookies with peanut butter inside. Oh, boy."

As he opened the box, he said, "I've been working as a janitor in a carpenter shop. Gives me a good chance to talk to people and pray with them. I've already made friends. Wes and Riley and John. We're thinking of having a Bible study. How are things with you?"

"Fine," said Holly. She told him about the Sunday and midweek church services she attended, about needlework she was doing with her mom, about Jared's interest in baseball.

"Great," enthused Monty. "I always liked baseball. One day soon I'm going to be out there helping my son in Little League. We'll trust God that it's soon."

There wasn't a lot more to say. Holly looked at her watch. Still an hour to go. Monty got out his Bible, and they compared Scriptures that the Lord had given each of them. Then it was time to leave.

Holly glanced at the guard and kissed Monty. "I'll see you tomorrow."

"I'll be here," Monty laughed. "And maybe bring me some grapes. Okay?"

Holly retraced her steps to the parking lot. The same procedure tomorrow and Sunday and in two weeks and two weeks after that...."Oh, God." She unlocked her car, noticing a group of women waiting at the bus stop. One woman came toward her.

"Say, you headin' back to Billings tonight? I need a ride."

"No," said Holly, "I'm not. Sorry. How did you know I'm from Billings?"

"Word gets around here pretty fast," said the woman. "If you're not goin', you must be stayin' at

Bill's?" The way she worded it, it was a question.

"Umm, no, I'm not. Who is Bill?"

The woman scrutinized Holly's car and nodded. "You're probably stayin' at a motel. Well, Honey, Bill's a kindly soul who lets wives and girlfriends stay in his house, free. He even baby-sits. Sure helps out when you got no money." She looked again at Holly's car. "Guess you don't need that, though." She walked back to the bus stop and talked to the others. They looked at Holly, and she heard, "Hotshot, huh?" loudly said.

Holly started the engine. Nothing would be easy.

Later she walked to a nearby restaurant. A nice dinner, then back to the motel for a good night's sleep. That's what I need, she thought, following the waitress.

Uniformed men clustered around tables. The kind of uniforms she saw today. Prison guards. Most looked up as she walked by, and she heard snatches of conversation. "Yeah, she's a waitin' woman. Saw her today."

When she was courageous enough to look up from her menu, she saw that most of the guards continued eating, but one, a paunchy, middle-aged man continued to stare at her, pursing his lips. Holly's skin crawled, and she ate quickly and paid her bill.

As she went out the door, she looked back. The guard ambled to the cash register and saluted his co-workers.

You're being silly, Holly told herself. There's nothing to worry about. Still she tried to walk faster without appearing to do so. She paused to look in a shop window and glanced around. He headed toward her with purposeful steps, a smile on his face. He really was following her.

There were two more blocks to her motel. She walked fast, her heart beating against her ribs. "Lord, where is my guardian angel?" She walked against the traffic light, hoping to be arrested. Out of breath, she reached her motel door, slammed, and locked it behind her. She burst into tears. "I can't do this. I can't."

* * *

The weeks piled on each other, centering around twice a month weekend visits to Deer Lodge. After the first scary guard incident, Holly always took the Afghans. They were allowed to stay in the motel. Even if they weren't ferocious, other people didn't know that. Jared went along most times. He'd bring a coloring book or schoolwork and sit quietly for the two-hour visiting time, content to look at his daddy once in awhile and to get a big hug and kiss.

Holly grew used to the grocery clerk's rudeness and the comments from the other wives and girl-friends. She became acquainted with a couple of them, so she had someone to talk to during the lonely hours in town. But the Friday excitement of seeing

Monty always spiraled down to a painful, heart-wrenching Sunday good-bye. The five-hour drive back to Billings was always made with her vision obscured by tears.

One day her friend said, "Holly, do you know that Isaiah 54:4 says that God will be a husband to those who have none? He will do the protecting and providing that a husband usually does."

Holly looked up the verse, and sighed. "There are so many things I don't know how to do—can't do, Lord. And I'm like a widow, so I claim this verse. You'll have to be the one to watch over me."

Holly couldn't get off work the following Friday. It was dark when she left for Deer Lodge. The thought crossed her mind to stop at the gas station. She looked at her fuel gauge. She didn't need gas, but was slowly learning that as God's child, those thoughts were usually from the Holy Spirit. She stopped.

"Ma'am," said the attendant. "I sure don't like the looks of your tires' treads. I'd like to rotate them for you. Free. Just don't want you to have a serious problem."

Holly checked the time. It would be midnight before she got to Deer Lodge, but okay.

A few minutes later, the attendant came around the hoist. "Good thing we looked at your tires. You had a nail. Looks like you've been driving on it quite awhile. Miracle you didn't have a blowout some-place."

Holly thought about the nine-hundred mile trip she made every other weekend. She'd never had a flat. "It was a miracle," she said.

But sometimes the evidence of God's working wasn't so noticeable. Often, Holly fell into the snare of dwelling on how long she would have to wait for Monty, how long she would have to travel to prison. Would her face become hardened like some of the other wives? "I know I'm committed to you Lord and to Monty, but does that mean I'm trapped for life?"

When the waiting and wondering and scariness became unbearable, she slipped back to her old habit of putting distance between herself and other Christians. They didn't understand. Not really. She felt she didn't belong in their happy, trusting groups. She knew she was doing it, but she didn't have the strength to combat it.

One evening she sat in the back of church so she could leave early. She didn't want to talk to people and didn't want to bump into the pastor's wife. During the altar call, she slipped out, and in the foyer ran smack into the pastor's wife.

"Holly, how's it going?" The pastor's wife put her hand on Holly's arm and looked earnestly into her face.

Holly pasted on a smile. "Just fine."

"Sure," said the other woman, knowingly. "You come up front and have Pastor pray for you. You need help and support, Holly. We love you."

No way out, thought Holly, allowing herself to be propelled to the altar. She sat, her head down, waiting for the pastor to finish praying for other people. She didn't know how to explain how she felt. What should she say that didn't sound as if she had no faith at all in God?

"Holly."

She looked up. The pastor bent over her, looking into her eyes. "Child, you're discouraged, aren't you?"

Suddenly Holly couldn't suppress all the loneliness and fear that had bubbled near the surface. She released them in a flow of tears.

The pastor said, "Something is really impressing my mind, Holly, and I believe it is from the Lord. It is that you've expected things to be smooth on your new road with Monty. You've expected the path to be straight. But there are many curves in that path and a few rocks in the way."

Holly nodded. She was disappointed in how things had turned out.

"And Holly," continued the pastor, "here's a Scripture for you. Psalm 37:5, 'Delight thyself in the Lord and He will give thee the desires of thine heart. Commit thy way unto the Lord, trust also in Him, and He shall bring it to pass.' "

Holly hugged the promise to herself all the way home. How wonderful to have Christian friends who loved and supported her. But most important, what a wonderful Lord who knew she hurt. Who knew her struggles, and was gently telling her to keep on trusting Him, to keep on believing that He would keep His promises.

"All right, Lord," she said. "I guess the ball is in Your heavenly court."

17

The Over the Wall in the Spirit Gang

Monty:

The dream—the vision of a prison ministry stayed with me. "I need another person to pray with me, to agree with me," I told the Lord. "Who will it be?"

John, my new cellmate, wasn't any help. He thought I was weird and barely tolerated me. I prayed harder. "Lord, You said a three-fold cord. You must have someone in mind."

Sometimes it was easier to tell Holly my feelings in a letter rather than in person.

> Honey, this place is becoming a blessing to me. It seems that once again, God is using me to minister His love and Holy Spirit to men here. God is moving in lives.

> Don't worry about me. I'm happy and content doing the Lord's work, or I should say, letting *Him* do His work in and through me.

I have a dream of a ministry here. Every day I'm going to encourage a group, which I will call "The Over the Wall in the Spirit Gang." Men will be able to share, pray, and study God's Word. Please ask the church to pray for all of us. I believe that if there are men gathered who are faithful, we will see a great move of the Spirit behind these walls. I'm excited.

Love, Monty

The day after I wrote this letter, John confronted me. "Okay, Christensen, I give up. I'm gettin' no rest. Everything I hear you say to the guys cuts me like a sharp knife. I want peace with God right now." He got down on his knees and waited for me to lead him in the sinner's prayer.

It took a moment to find my voice. "Ahh...sure, John." Wow. This blew me away.

The next day, John's wife came to see him. John came back to the cell flying high. "Told my wife what I did and that she needed God too, and guess what? I led her in the same prayer you said with me. Right there at the table. Our kids are next."

I shook my head in amazement. "God, I guess You sent the third part of the cord."

* * *

John, Wes, Riley, Don, and myself made up the nucleus of the O.W.S. Gang. Every day at three o-clock, we gathered in John's and my cell, sharing and studying. Other men, intrigued by what was happening, joined us. Lamar, growing in the Word, was a regular.

As some church people do, and certainly as I had, inmates also have preconceived ideas about Christians. One day on the catwalk Riley confronted me.

"Monty, you went to prison, found the Lord, got out of prison, and then came back. Real Christians don't do bad things. I don't think a real Christian would be back in prison. So I'm wondering why you're leading our group."

I had mulled that over in my mind a lot. Satan whipped me over the head with it, and I finally knew the answer.

"Riley, it doesn't make any difference who you are or how long you've known the Lord. It's possible to fall prey to Satan's traps. And, Riley, the Bible speaks to that. It says, 'take heed if you think you stand, lest you fall.' "

Riley's look said he wasn't about to listen, and he stomped off.

Two days later, John said, "Hear about poor Riley? He and a guard got into it over something, and Riley threatened to hurt him. He's in solitary."

I felt no satisfaction in hearing that. Riley was another Christian having a painful experience.

"Come on," I said. "We can't let a wounded Christian die. Let's pray."

It's possible to fall into Satan's traps, but the Lord's mighty arm will free us. Riley learned about God's unending forgiveness.

Holly wrote me about her struggles to keep from the yo-yo syndrome. One day everything's fine, the next, discouragement hits. Some of my letters to her reflected my own struggles in that area. But because of my constant opportunity to minister—whether leading someone to Christ or comforting a brother whose parole didn't come through—most of the time I could cheer her up.

Holly, tonight I'm enjoying a blessed peace deep in my heart. It hurts that we're separated, but I hope that we can both see the hand of God on our lives. We're learning more of His ways. We're learning the patience and endurance that He can use to minister to others.

Ooops, excuse me a minute, Holly. The guards are shaking down my cell. They can't quite figure me out. They think I must be smoking some kind of dope, because I seem to be joyous, so they do this often. I just hope they don't throw any of my pictures out. I'm possessive of my pictures of you and Jared.

Anyway, if you're down today, you might pretend you're here beside me and together we see God's hand in our lives. He is preparing us for a total walk in faith. He wants that faith in us because it will move mountains.

Only He knows what comes next, but He has a plan and a work for us as a team.

I love you—

The younger Christians, barely out of their teens, were a ministry by themselves. Their lack of experience age-wise, as well as in the Lord, made them vulnerable. Several of them worked in the kitchen with Satan worshippers, including the head of the prison cult.

The satanists had a star on their cell floors and read the black book, their "bible" written by my old housemate, Anton. While we prayed and sang praises to God, they worshipped the darkness in their own cells. And that darkness could be forceful.

"Monty," the young Christians said, "Those guys said Satan will give us power and money and things. More than God."

"Hey," I said, "you know better than that. Satan's a liar."

But it kept up, and one day I got fed up. Mad. I went to our Over-the-Wall-in-the-Spirit Gang. "Okay, there's only one thing to do. Pray and believe for these satanists' salvation."

We prayed. And we prayed. We bound Satan and his demons in Jesus' name, and we prayed some more. Two weeks later, the head of the prison satanists appeared in the chapel. He accepted Jesus!

God was on the move in the Deer Lodge Penitentiary. Over the ensuing weeks, all the prison leaders—all of them—came to my cell. The Indian leader; Grady, the black leader; Reed, a homosexual who prostituted young men in prison; the drug dealers— they all came, secretly, looking over their shoulders. "Monty, I got to talk to you."

I listened to them, pointed the way to Jesus, and prayed with them. They always felt better when they left, and although I never saw any fruits of those secret meetings, I prayed that seeds were planted.

* * *

The chaplain came to see me. "Monty, how would you like to give a message at the prison brotherhood group Friday night? Don't get too emotional, though."

I couldn't believe he had asked me. I had never preached a sermon. My words would get all mixed up. What would I say?

"Aah...sure...." I stammered. I was committed.

I went to the Lord in a panic. His calm voice said, "Tell them about you. About your struggles. And how My forgiveness is unending."

I did. I shared my own story, and I said, "A lot of you are the same. Maybe your parents stuffed your emotions. You couldn't cry or get angry. So you wouldn't allow those emotions to function in your life.

"In your teen years you experimented with drugs and alcohol. You needed a place to feel accepted and loved. You got a little buzz on the beer or the drug. For the first time in your life, you could release those emotions. You felt good. The drug did a good thing. But down the road, the drug became a chain. You were in bondage. It took you over. Then Satan moved in and worked in those areas of your life. Right?"

There were a few nods of agreement. The joy in me of what I was about to say, nearly overwhelmed me, and it exploded from my mouth.

"But God knows that. He knows why you are who you are. And it doesn't matter. He loves you. You're special to Him. Don't let Satan tell you there's a limit to God's forgiveness. He tried that on me. God's forgiveness goes beyond—beyond everything."

I turned to sit down. Did my talk do any good? Then as one, thirty men jumped out of their chairs, hugging each other, crying, shouting praises to the Lord.

The chaplain came to a front chair and knelt. "Oh, God, become more real to me," he cried. I put my arm around him and cried with him.

That night, in my cell, I lay on my face before God. How could the mighty, awesome God, the creator of the universe—Who could wipe away the world with a thought—love me so much? Love me enough to take my punishment? Then allow me to be used in His important work?

It blew my mind to think about it. And even if I

spent the rest of my life in prison, I would be grateful for that love.

18

God and a Man Called Tex

Part One

Monty: Winter, 1979

In spite of the excitement of doing God's work, I struggled with apprehension and the fear that always tags on. Idaho and New Mexico deferred to Oregon's charges. At least I didn't have those anymore, but the prospect of forty years in an Oregon prison brought sweat to my forehead.

My attorney still worked on the chance of lessening the sentence, but offered no hope. Holly's every-two-week visits encouraged and brightened my life, but she was scared, too.

Pastor Bob frequently wrote me. Often he was the only person to whom I could bare my fears and frustrations.

"Monty," he said, "God's brought you a long way. Do you think He'll drop you now?"

So I hung on to that and to every promise God had

given me. Still it was hard. A letter came from Holly.

> Monty, I feel the problem of getting great things from God is being able to hold on for the last hour. Somehow, amid the discouragement, there will be a victory. I feel strongly that it won't be long until we're together. Maybe even by next week. The hardest part is near the end. Keep trusting.

Satan did some skywriting in my mind. Holly and I sure mouth a lot of platitudes. Whistling in the dark. I've got to serve every last year of my sentence. I deserve it.

But then God's promise in Ezekiel 34, the one He gave to both Holly and me, overrode the con. I was learning that the only way to fight Satan was with the Word.

One day I sat in my cell struggling with self-pity, when the sergeant of the guards came in and handed me official papers. I scanned them and looked at him in bewilderment. "These can't be real. It must be a joke."

"No joke. They're real."

"But it says Oregon has dropped all its charges. Every one. How...? Who...?" I was so dumbfounded I didn't know what to ask.

"I don't know," said the guard. "I only deliver. I can tell you, though, you'll be leaving close-custody and going up to minimum security."

After he left, I yelled, "I'm getting out of here!

John, I'm really getting out of prison. All charges dropped. Thank you, God. Boy, John, God sure pulls some good ones." I stopped suddenly, remembering that John had three ten-year sentences for embezzlement stacked against him.

"Monty, that's great," he said, clasping my hand. "God is able to do great things above all that we ask or expect. I'm trusting Him for my life, too."

I had to call Holly. I ran to a phone. "Holly, guess what? No, you'll never guess. Montana and Oregon dropped all charges. I'll be getting out! Our attorney was working on getting lesser charges. I don't know how he managed to pull this off."

"I know, Monty. I got off the phone with him just before you called." Holly was laughing. "It's wonderful. But he didn't do it. He had nothing to do with it. He was notified as a matter of course."

"What...? What...? How...?" My bewilderment came across on the phone.

"Monty, he said Pastor Bob has been working behind the scenes."

"Bob?" I couldn't believe it. He'd never said a word. Besides, what clout did he have? And to get all the charges dropped when an attorney couldn't?

"I don't know all the details," Holly said. "Something about a man named Tex. You'll have to ask Bob."

I hung up, feeling deliriously happy, but baffled. What was going on? Tex? Tex who?

* * *

I called Pastor Bob fast. "What's going on?"

"Sorry for the seeming subterfuge, Monty, but I wasn't sure how it would work and thought it best to keep quiet." He paused and I waited. "I've watched you," he continued, "and we've talked. I believe your conversion is solid. I believe you're on solid footing and growing. And I believe that God has special plans for you. So with all this in mind I wrote to a friend, Tex Rutledge, who is dean of students at Northwest College in Kirkland, Washington."

"Yeah," I impatiently tapped my fingers on the side of the telephone box.

Pastor Bob must have heard, for he laughed. "I'm getting to it. Tex used to work with the Oregon Correctional Systems as a consultant and counselor. I told him about you, and asked if he could help. He called Oregon, made a few inquiries, and bingo."

"But this Tex has never met me. He did that sight unseen?"

"He hasn't seen you with his own eyes, Monty, that's true. But Tex relies heavily on the witness of the Holy Spirit. And he got a go-ahead."

That night in the cell, I said to John, "You know the Bible verse that says 'God works in mysterious ways'? Well, boy, it's true."

* * *

Minimum security was a farm. I traded in my prison khakis for jeans and blue shirts and went to work. The quarters were nicer than the old prison, and there was more freedom. But I was isolated from my friends. From the O.W.S. gang. I missed the daily mundane things like walking and talking with a friend in the yard—the basketball—but mostly, the ministry.

There were other Christians there, one I knew from brotherhood meetings, but the spark wasn't there. We had more freedom for church services, but the men weren't as interested as before. It hit home that people pray and seek God more when under the whip.

I tried not to let it bother me. After all, I would leave in a week or so.

The guard was a new Christian with terrific marriage problems. He welcomed the chance to pray with another Christian. Sometimes in the field or riding in the truck, we'd read Scripture. At that point, he was the only Christian fellowship I had.

The "week or so" stretched. More than a month went by. I had continual meetings with the parole board. They couldn't seem to make up their minds. Holly and I were both discouraged. They could keep this up indefinitely. We kept the mails busy.

Hi, Honey. Today I charged across the field, full speed on my tractor, pitch fork in hand like a spear, chasing a coyote. He outran me, but sure had me going. Of course, the great hunter, I'm not.

My boss and I had a long talk, with prayer. Times like that make me feel guilty because I'm leaving. I see I'm needed. His pastor told him to divorce his wife if she doesn't shape up. He doesn't want that, and now knows what the Bible says. I sure love this guy and don't think divorce is the answer. He's beginning to trust my judgment a little, which is major, because I'm a con and he's a cop.

It's neat to take care of a big field and watch the grass grow green and tall. I irrigate about two hundred acres, but I can sing and praise the Lord to my heart's content out there. Waiting for the water, I also get plenty of reading time. It's a living experience. Praise God for nature to show His ways.

Tonight I went to a Yoke Fellow meeting. It was a blessing. I can see God working in other lives here, but He's mostly dealing with me.

Sweetheart, this has been hard on both of us. "But in all things, give thanks, for this is the will of God concerning you." Don't mean to preach, but that's hit home. We've needed the time I've been in prison to re-establish our relationship. We've needed the time to talk, a kind of safety zone. We couldn't have done it on the streets. I hate to think what would have happened. So thank God for His ways. I love you.

It happened fast. The posted "movement" sheet listed who had doctor appointments, who was going to school, and occasionally who was being released. I scanned it on my way to the field. Holly would be there that afternoon, and I didn't want anything interfering.

There was my name. "Monty Christensen—released Monday."

Monday—two days. I couldn't wait to tell Holly.

Part Two

Holly:

I will never get used to this, Holly said to herself. Minimum security is really no different. She sat down in the visiting room and looked around. The women's faces did seem to be more cheerful here, but how much longer? She smoothed her pink and white dress.

Monty burst through the door, a grin from ear to ear.

"You've been released," Holly squealed. "When?"

"Monday. Holly, that's day after tomorrow. Will you come get me? And oh...I need clothes. And...I'm sorry, Honey, I'm excited...but I heard there's a Hungry Horse Bible Camp by Glacier Park. We could go and make it sort of a honeymoon. Do you think you could get time off?"

Holly thought she might burst with joy. "Oh, that sounds wonderful. Yes, oh, yes. I'll take my vacation. I'll go home first thing tomorrow and buy you some clothes. Pink slacks and purple shirt okay?"

"Very funny." Monty kissed her. "Hurry, but be careful."

Holly ran to her car, mentally making a list. Call the office, check out of the motel in the morning, drive home, buy Monty's clothes, pack her stuff, call Mom to take Jared, water the plants, dogs to the kennel. Back again tomorrow night. Oh, no, could she do it all?

She sang the whole way to Billings. The drive never seemed as fast.

Get into high gear, she admonished herself as soon as she hit her front door. Somehow it all got done, and Monday morning she gave Monty's clothes to the guard.

"Pick him up at the guard tower. About an hour," he said.

She headed there and sat waiting, remembering the first visiting day when the woman said, "Hurry up and wait. Hurry up and wait."

It's sure true, Holly thought. Scenes from the past months flicked across her mind.

"Thank you, Jesus, for going through it with me," she said. "Thank you for paying the bills. Thank you for looking after my tires. Thank you for being a husband."

The door in the tower opened. Monty stood there, looking around uncertainly, his new clothes a contrast to the drabness around him.

Holly waved and honked as he came running, a small bag bouncing at his side. They embraced. "What took so long?" asked Holly.

"It took ages for the guards to bring me the clothes, and then I couldn't seem to get them on. Too much in a hurry, I guess. Do you want me to drive?"

"You bet," Holly said, moving to the passenger's side. "Take over."

Two miles out of town, the car swerved. Monty pulled to a stop. "We've got a flat tire," he announced.

"No!" Holly covered her mouth so he couldn't see her smile. "Honey, I'm so glad I have a husband to take care of it."

* * *

Holly enjoyed the camp. I'm glad we have something like this to fill our time, she thought. After the first excitement of Monty's release, she realized she really didn't know this man beside her anymore. She didn't know how to talk to him when it was just the two of them. He's a stranger, she admitted. And he probably feels the same way about me.

Fifteen minutes into the camp's first session, Monty gasped and ran out of the building. Holly ran after him. "What's wrong?"

Monty leaned against a wall, breathing hard. When he could speak, he said, "I don't know. I got claustrophobia or something. I couldn't breathe. I had to get out of there."

After a few minutes, he went back in, only to have the same attack later.

What's wrong with him? He never used to do that, Holly inwardly cried. He's different. We've both changed. It was clear they had another struggle ahead. Could they make it?

At one session, the couple next to them introduced themselves. Dick and Sharon, friends of Monty's former boss, who were from Bellevue, Washington.

"Is that near Northwest Bible College?" Monty asked. "I really want to go to Bible college."

"It's practically next door," said Dick. "And there's a neat church. Come visit. Stay with us."

"Well...I just got out of prison." Monty spoke hesitantly, as though expecting a rebuff.

"Congratulations," said Dick.

"Do plan on staying with us," his wife added to Holly.

"Thank you," Holly said quietly. She forgot her worries of the afternoon. The Lord seemed to be paving the way, showing them the path. All she and Monty had to do was follow.

✤ ✤ ✤

19

New Place-Old Struggles-
New End

Part One

Monty: Summer, 1979

After the Bible camp, I got a construction job in Billings. But I had slipped into prison dependency—used to having someone else make my decisions. Sometimes choosing the right size nail overwhelmed me. It was painful. My self-image took a beating.

"The Lord wants me to go to Bible school anyway," I said to Holly one bad day.

Her mom took Jared, and we accepted Dick and Sharon's hospitality offer and went to Washington State to find a job and a place to live. From prison to freedom may be a culture shock, but it is nothing like going from a small Montana town to high-tech Bellevue, Washington.

We couldn't believe the prices. We had the end of Holly's insurance money, about fifteen hundred dollars, but after pounding the pavement, going from one realtor to another, we found nothing that would allow us to eat after paying the rent. All the job opportunities demanded resumes and references, and politely closed when confronted with my last residence.

Our friends took us to a service at the Neighborhood Church. Holly and I had never felt such love in a church; and after going out afterwards for ice cream with Pastor and Mrs. Rozell, we felt at home. But the problems of finding work and a place to live seemed insurmountable.

One afternoon after a fruitless search, we headed back to our hosts' home. Neither of us said a word. At a stoplight I rested my head on the steering wheel and said, "Holly, I goofed. God doesn't want us here. All I've done is waste our money. Let's go home tomorrow."

She sighed. "I guess you're right, but I'm hungry. Let's have a last meal."

Over our beef stroganoff we struggled to make cheerful conversation. As I paid the check, I glanced at a row of newspaper boxes. "Hey, we haven't tried the classifieds," I said.

I spoke to a passerby. "Excuse me, which newspaper is best to check for a house to rent?"

She pointed to one, but said, "I have a realtor friend. Why don't you call her?" At our hesitation, she added, "I don't know if it makes any difference to you, but she's a Christian."

Holly and I looked at each other and smiled. "It

sure does make a difference," we said at the same time.

At the first house, the agent said, "The owners have prayed for Christian tenants."

This must be where we are meant to be, I thought. I decided to be honest about our situation. "We can't move right in. We have loose ends to tie up back home, and I...I need to get a parole transfer."

I waited for the look I had seen on prospective employers' faces.

"No problem," she said. "Leave a deposit and come when you're ready."

In Billings we found the dogs a home where they could run. A month later, we packed Jared and our possessions in the car and drove over snowy passes back to Bellevue. The move took all our money. We could afford to heat only one room in the house, so we camped in the living room—Jared in his bed and Holly and I in sleeping bags on the floor.

A week after moving in, I still had no job. Old tapes began to whir. "Nothing you touch ever turns out right....God won't bless you....You've failed too many times....You were never meant to be anything but a failure .... You can't face anyone .... Run .... Forget...."

Because of the shock to my system from the change in my life, I was still too weak to function, much less fight off Satan's attacks or go for help. I've since decided that persons coming off drugs and alcohol should wait a year before making major decisions about their lives, and then at least three years before considering going into the ministry. Practical things need to be worked out. Those getting out of an institution should wait three years. When a seedling isn't grounded in deep soil, with strong roots, it withers and dies. I wasn't strong, and my life needed maturity, growth, and balancing. But like others, I didn't like the word wait. After all, God called me...So when I fell over, I threw in the towel.

"Holly, you want to go with me? I'm going out and get drunk."

Part Two

Holly: September

As Monty's words sank in, Holly felt as if a ton of sand were being dumped inside her. Slowly it filled each crevice, rising higher and higher until she felt its weight in her throat, and she couldn't breathe or speak. She shook her head, not knowing what to say.

After what seemed an eternity, she forced words through her dry mouth, "Sharon and Dick will be here in the morning to take us to garage sales."

"I'm not going." Monty hunched into his jacket. "If you're not coming with me—see ya."

She heard the car screech down the street, and she ran to the door, pounding her fists against its solidness. "No...not again. He's doing it to me again."

She spent the night listening for him, crying, and dozing. It was four in the morning when he returned and collapsed on top of his sleeping bag.

A few hours later, the door bell awakened her. Sharon and Dick, she thought. They can't see us like this. Monty snored on. She raised a cautioning finger to Jared not to open the door and held her breath.

After awhile, their friends' car drove away. Holly buried her head in her hands. She and Monty were again withdrawing, alienating themselves from support. "I can't believe this is happening," she cried.

She didn't want to have to talk to Monty when he awakened. She and Jared drove to the shopping mall. When they returned a few hours later, Monty was gone.

From the top of her head, black depression settled like a blanket, swirling around and around until it collided with the heaviness in her chest.

Get help, Holly, she ordered herself. She'd call the pastor of the church that she and Monty visited. After all, the pastor of her small-town church had always been available. She remembered when she called him at six in the morning to tell him Monty was coming home.

"I'm sorry," said the receptionist, "but Pastor has a funeral this afternoon. And he's booked up with counseling for the next few days. After that we could make an appointment or get you into our lay counseling program sooner."

"Never mind." Holly hung up. No one would help her. It isn't the pastor's fault, she said to herself. It's a big church—must be lots of people with problems. But she couldn't bring herself to talk to anyone else but a pastor.

You and God did it before, a thought reminded. "Yeah," she said, "so why do I have to go through this again? It isn't fair."

A couple of days later, her mother called. "Holly, I've been to the doctor, and I have incurable cancer."

A chilling numbness settled around Holly's heart.

"The doctor thinks I should go to a medical center in Seattle," her mother continued. "So I'm moving, but will need help. Can you come?"

"Mom, I wish I could, but I don't have the money to get back there." Holly suddenly felt like throwing up. What was she supposed to do?

"I can get someone else. See you in a couple of weeks," her mother ended the conversation.

Holly burst into tears. Mom, the one person in her life to whom she could always turn. Mom was dying. The thought was overwhelming. Monty had rejected her again and now her mom. She had no one. Somewhere she had heard that stress triggered cancer. She was the one who had given her mother stress. She was killing her mother. Her sobs turned to whimpers. "I want to die," she whispered.

The door blew open and Jared, cheeks and nose red from the cold, rolled his baseball across the floor.

"Hi, Mom."

She looked at him through swollen eyelids. Jared needed her. With determination she dialed the Neighborhood Church. "I'd like an appointment with a counselor," she said, her voice shaking. "Day after tomorrow? Fine." She sank down in the room's only chair. That one decision used up all her strength.

The day of the counseling session, Holly sat fidgeting in the waiting room. She had used every ounce of energy to keep the appointment. She could leave even now.

"Holly, come in." The director of the lay-counseling ushered her into his office. "Tell me what's wrong."

"My husband is ripping me apart with his drinking and drugs. He's supposed to be a Christian. We've been through this so many times. I can't handle it anymore. Why does he do this to me? I'm so depressed." She erupted in sobs.

The counselor listened a few minutes, then drew two circles on a sheet of paper. "Holly, this one circle is you. The other one, Monty. You have been totally absorbed in Monty, your relationship, everything that has to do with Monty's circle. But that's his circle. What he does shouldn't affect you. You're a separate individual with a separate identity and a separate set of problems. You need to work on yours, like your self-pity, and let the Lord take care of Monty."

"Self-pity?" Holly dabbed a tissue at her eyes and

looked at him in amazement. Didn't he hear what she had said? Monty was the one with the problems. She was the victim. Why was the counselor picking on her?

He looked at her kindly. "Let's list a few of the things going on inside you. We can certainly say that you feel resentful toward Monty. Right?"

"Of course," she responded, and he wrote resentment.

"Bitterness?"

She nodded. "I guess so."

"And who do you think is being hurt by his actions?"

"I am," Holly said softly. She could almost feel a physical impact from the words. That's what he meant. She felt sorry for herself.

The counselor turned the paper around so she could read it, and said quietly, "In God's eyes, these are equal to Monty's sins. When you go home, check to see what Hebrews 12:15 says. Also Ephesians 4:31 and 32, Matthew 6:14 and 15, and Romans 12:14."

He wrote the references at the bottom of the page. "I'm also writing down some other homework for you to do before your next appointment." He put his hand on Holly's shoulder. "You made it through the first step. Everything will be okay."

Holly left, feeling calmer. At home, she sat down with her Bible and looked up the references. "Root of bitterness...." "Forgiving one another...." "Forgive men their trespasses...." "Be not overcome by evil, but overcome evil with good...."

God had a lot to say about her feelings. She knew it was easier to blame Monty for the things he did that could be seen on the outside. But she always thought she was a good person. She went to church, did the right things and got in the habit of looking at Monty as bad. But while her sins weren't so obvious, they were indeed sins.

"Lord, I need changing. Change me," she cried. How would He do it?

At the next appointment, Holly had a new counselor, a Mrs. Miller. After they talked awhile, the counselor said, "Holly, in order for you to change, we need to learn why you're taking these 'poor-me pills.' There must be a payoff in it for you."

"A payoff? What do you mean?"

"Perhaps, Holly, as a child, when you were sick or depressed, people paid attention to you. Sometimes they gave negative attention, but at least they did it. You were 'paid' for taking the 'poor-me pills.' Could that be true?"

"Yes," said Holly thoughtfully. "The only time my mom paid attention to me was when she felt sorry for me. And thinking about it, I see that when Monty left me, people felt sorry for me. The attention made me feel good. I guess I had pity parties and invited everyone to share my 'poor-me pills,' as you call them."

"Smart girl," said Mrs. Miller. "What would happen if you threw away the bottle of pills?"

"I don't know," said Holly. "People wouldn't pay attention to me, and that's...."

"Frightening?" You wouldn't have anything to put in its place? Do you know what God says about fear?"

"His perfect love casts it out?"

"Yes, He comes in and sweeps it out. Also in Isaiah 41:10 He says—here, you read it, Holly, and insert your own name."

Holly began to read. "Fear not, for I am with Holly. Do not be dismayed; I am Holly's God. I will strengthen Holly. I will help Holly. I will uphold Holly with my victorious right hand." She looked up. "He did it before, so He can do it again. I guess I can trust Him."

"Then let's pray that God will set you free."

"Dear Father," Holly's voice quivered with emotion. "I've held resentment and bitterness against Monty—and by having self-pity, I've put myself on the throne instead of You. I confess these things as sins and ask You to forgive me. Remind me, Lord, to love Monty and not to let those sins get a foothold anymore. I'm letting go, and I trust You to uphold me as You promised. Thank You. In Jesus' name, amen."

"You're on your way," said the counselor. "Now let's see what Pastor Rozell and a Christian psychiatrist say about your depression."

The following day Holly swallowed a prescribed antidepressant pill. This will help, she thought. I'll keep rejecting self-pity and resentment, and these will help me do it. How wonderful to be feeling good again.

Part Three

Monty:

It was the morning after the night before. I rolled over in my sleeping bag and groaned. I knew I deserved to feel sick. Why was I doing this stuff? Every morning for the past four weeks I looked in the bathroom mirror and asked the same question. I didn't want to keep on with drugs and booze, but I couldn't stop.

This particular morning Holly sang in the kitchen. The noise, although soft, blasted my eardrums and made me sicker at heart. I knew she had gone for help for her depression. She was strong enough to do that, and here I was. I hated myself.

Before I lost my nerve, I got in the car and drove to the local alcohol center. "I guess I need help," I said to the receptionist.

She introduced me to a counselor who talked to me, then said, "Monty, come to our meeting tonight. You may learn some surprising things."

Meetings? No way. I wanted someone to say

magic words to give me willpower. I backed out ten times in my mind that afternoon. But after remembering how I hated myself each morning, I downed a beer and went.

The counselor was right. I learned things that surprised me.

"Holly," I said when I got home that night, "do you know what you're looking at? An alcoholic and a drug addict. Can you believe it?"

"An addict?" Holly made a face. "You used to take the stuff a lot, but this time you haven't been on it as long. Besides, you're too young. Addicts are old guys on skid road, aren't they?"

I shrugged. "Guess not. At the meeting they said that less than three percent of alcoholics were on the street. The rest are here in suburbia. I'm an addict. That blows me away. Holly, I learned so much tonight. They said there's hope for me. I can't wait to go back. Listen, you want to go to church Sunday?"

* * *

On Sunday, Pastor Rozell stood inside the sanctuary doors as we accepted a church bulletin from a smiling greeter.

"Holly, Monty, Jared. It's great to see you." He grabbed us all in a family hug.

The sermon was in-depth teaching from the

Word. The pastor spoke on how anxiety and stress can be used for growth. It was meant for Holly and me. I shook my head in awe. I felt I was at a Thanksgiving table loaded with good, rich food.

"Let the Holy Spirit speak to you about your heart attachment," the pastor said at the conclusion. "Are you thinking His thoughts? Are your affections attached securely to Him? Is your will directed to His purpose? Is the Person on the throne mastering your life?"

The part about my will directed to God's purpose zapped me. God had called me to preach the gospel. I had better get on with it. I glanced at Holly. She was weeping softly, but nodding her head as if in affirmation of a new understanding.

The bulletin listed a meeting time for the "Amen" group, an alcoholic-support group. I nudged Holly and pointed to it. "Think I'll go," I whispered.

I had also promised Holly I would have a physical. The next day the doctor said, "Monty, you have a chemical imbalance. I'll prescribe lithium. It's expensive, but you need it."

The mineral made me feel better, but now both Holly and I were on expensive medications, and I had only a part-time construction job. I tried to push that from my mind in my elation over our new-found church. The "Amen" group allowed me the wonderful feeling of bouncing off others who I was, and where I was, and see their responses. No one condemned me for slipping back into bondage three times after becoming a Christian.

Soon every time the church doors opened, I was there—hungry for the Word and fellowship. This was the first church where it was okay to be me. I relaxed.

Yet sometimes I felt angry at the people sitting there so comfortably. Our family needed help. Why didn't they care? They weren't treating us the way Jesus would.

But then slowly the realization dawned that I wasn't their judge. That I could show them the love I thought they should show me. I could reach out and tell them our need. They weren't mind readers. I shared our circumstances and gave my last five-dollar bill to another man who was also having problems.

One cold, rainy Saturday during our morning devotions, Holly and I read "Delight yourself in the Lord; and He will give you the desires of your heart." (Ps. 37:4)

"We have to remember that," Holly said. "That's a promise."

Later that day I was in the garage trying to find out what was wrong with the car when she wandered in. "Brr," she shivered. "It's gloomy. Wouldn't a bowl of hot chili taste good?"

"Sure would." I stretched my head around the open car hood. "Got the fixings?"

"Not hardly," she laughed. "Just wishin'. We've got peanut butter and eggs for dinner."

An hour later, there was a knock on the door. A lady we had seen at church handed us a sack with two loaves of bread on top and said, "Just stopped by with some bread for you. Hope you can use it."

After she left, Holly unpacked the sack. "Monty," she squealed in delight, "look!" In the bottom of the sack was a package of ground beef, tomato sauce—everything you needed to make chili.

"The desires of your heart!" we both shouted at once.

Pastor Rozell learned we had no beds, so his family gave us one of theirs. I began watching him—how he functioned as a husband, a father, and a member of the community. He was the first positive image I had ever had.

Three months later, Holly and I were on our way out of the woods. As we focused on our individual walks with God, we were amazed how our walks with each other were a lot closer—like a pyramid with God at the top. As we both went toward Him, we grew closer, and noticed changes in each other. Holly no longer said to me in words and actions, "You're the big bad sinner, and I'm the good saint."

However, much of our well-being depended on our medication. One night I said to the Lord, "God, I can't afford to buy these pills anymore. You'll have to totally heal me. I won't take any more."

Financially there was no way around my having to step out in faith for healing, and God over the next few weeks healed me from my deficiency.

Holly still took her drug which made her tongue so thick she could hardly talk. One day she said, "I'm mad. I know Satan is still trying to destroy me. I feel out of control. If I had moved the steering wheel a little today, I would have driven off the road. And I got panicky in the grocery store. I feel like a walking zombie most of the time. You got healed, Monty, so I told God He would have to do the same for me. I won't take this anymore—I'm through with tranquilizers."

I took her hand. "Lord," I prayed, "we've both stepped out on Your promise limb, but we know we won't crash because You are faithful to Your Word. Thank You for healing our bodies, and our emotions, and for getting us on course for Your purpose."

* * *

Everytime we think we're on top, we fall flat. I got laid off my part-time job, but when Satan started grinding out the old death marches, Holly and I told him to take a flying leap. Our God was faithful.

The next week at the men's prayer meeting, the pastor introduced me to Wilbur Vorhees who said, "Monty, I hear you need a job. I have a construction company, and I'd like to hire you to do subcontracting. Of course, you'll have to get a contractor's license, but you'll be making...." He named a sum that took my breath away.

I wanted to go right home to tell Holly, but the men were going out to breakfast and invited me to go. I looked at Wilbur Vorhees as we drove. Distinguished and kind looking, probably my father's age. My boss. How would I handle it? I still had a problem with authority images—guards, cops, pastors.

In the restaurant booth, the men introduced themselves. The big, powerfully built guy across from me said, "I'm John. I'm a police officer."

My stomach turned upside down, and the hair on the back of my neck stood up. I hated him on the spot, because I knew how pigheaded cops think. I knew what they were like. He couldn't be a Christian.

I got through the sausage and eggs and went home to tell Holly the good news about the job, determined to stay far away from John the cop. If he was going to be a prayer meeting regular, I might not go anymore.

In the afternoon the phone rang. "Monty, this is John. Remember me? You know, I think we have a lot in common. I found out from Pastor where you live, and I wondered if I could come over tonight and meet your family? I'll bring pizza."

"Uh...uh...well..."

"If tonight's no good, how about tomorrow?"

"Okay, okay." I didn't know what to say. "Come tonight."

At seven o'clock that evening, my heart flip-flopped as a police siren moaned its way down our street and died in front of our house. Holly and I ran to the window. A squad car, lights throbbing, sat outside. As we stared, horror-struck, a powerful spotlight shone through our picture window and blinked seven times in a friendly staccato.

"Hi," John said as we opened the door. "The pizza's getting cold."

Twice a week, lonely John, going through hard places in his life, delighted Jared by pulling the same routine as he arrived for a sharing time, dessert, or dinner. The neighbors got used to it, and I began to see that through God's sense of humor, a healing started in my heart about authority figures. John turned out to be my best friend.

* * *

Holly's mother got a small apartment in our area, and Holly took her to treatments. Holly hated to see her in pain, but her mom enjoyed being with Jared again, and we were all on a new relationship basis.

We planned a trip to Oregon to see Uncle Truman. Knowing she couldn't make the trip in a car, we borrowed a friend's R.V., and she lay on the bed playing word games with Jared and Holly. At Christmas time we sang carols as we drove around seeing the lights. We gave her a Bible, which made her cry.

"Holly, Monty, this is a wonderful Christmas. God is good. Whatever happens to me, I know you two will make it." She touched my arm, a gesture she had never made before.

* * *

I thought a lot about restitution. The Old Testament edict about stealing a cow and paying back two is valid. I had already contacted all the people I could whom I had hurt. I asked my grandmother's forgiveness for forging her check, and before she died, had gradually won back her confidence. Most forgiveness came over a period of time as people saw that I was "walking it out."

I put Mrs. Moser through a lot of pain, but the night before she died, she called me from her hospital bed. "Monty, I want you to know that we both know the same Jesus. I love you, Monty."

"I love you, too," I said, meaning it from the bottom of my heart.

Part Four

Holly: Winter, 1980

"I feel like an orphan," Holly confided to a friend. "My dad is gone, and now Mom. I ache inside. I remember all the things I put her through. Old thoughts are continually hitting me—like I'll hurt everyone I love, so why not take myself out of the picture?"

243

"You know that's a lie of Satan's, Holly," responded her friend. "Don't let him do that to you. You need prayer support. Why don't you and Monty come with me to a special service at my church?"

"I'd like that," said Holly. "I do need prayer for my leg. It's never been the same since my accident."

At the service the congregation sang a song based on Isaiah 53:5.

"...and by His wounds we are healed."

Holly stretched her arm toward heaven. "God, I'm taking you at Your word."

She got in the prayer line intending to mention her leg, but the minister looked earnestly at her. "Young lady, don't be afraid. I'm going to pray over you."

He said something about breaking the power of the spirit of death. "That's strange," Holly thought. "Wonder what that has to do with my leg?"

When she returned to her seat and told Monty, he hugged her. "Holly, do you suppose that meant your suicidal inclinations? For years you've been harassed to take your life."

The following week she related the incident to her friend. "You know, since Mom died, I've had constant thoughts about suicide, but haven't had one since I was prayed for. Jesus healed me."

* * *

"Holly, you know, it's great to be in God's will," Monty said one spring day. "I'm sharing my testimony, making a fabulous salary, and we are able to help support different ministries."

Holly smiled and opened a just-arrived letter. As she read, a lump grew in her throat. She handed the letter to Monty. "It's from Lamar's wife, Emily. Remember, you led him to the Lord in jail, and he went to the penitentiary before you did. I saw her in the waiting room."

"Sure, I remember. You saw her in church after that, and she said she had also given her heart to the Lord. What does she say? How's Lamar?" Monty took the closely written page and read:

I don't know if you remember me, but I think of you often and pray for you.

In case you didn't hear, my husband, Lamar, was murdered in his room at the state prison. His throat was cut. A lot of evidence was sent to the state crime lab, but no official decisions have been made as to why or who.

Praise God Lamar died in Jesus, and praise God, he won't be cold this winter. He was always so cold at the prison.

I miss him, but the Lord loves me and I keep busy. Thank you for listening and understanding and caring when Lamar was in prison.

P.S. Here's ten dollars for you, Holly. It's a present from the Lord.

Tears streamed down Holly's cheeks. "I never realized I did anything for her. And Monty...if you hadn't led Lamar to Jesus...."

Part Five

Monty:

I bowed my head over the letter, not praying, not even thinking. Just waiting. I was enjoying my life—what I thought God wanted me to do—being a Christian businessman. But a week before, Wilbur Vorhees had made an unsettling comment.

"Monty, I want you to keep working here, but I'm concerned that by giving you a job, I may be keeping you from doing what God really wants you to do."

I had pushed that out of my mind, but here was this letter, hitting me in the heart with what I was supposed to be doing—leading other Lamars and their murderers to the Lord. I decided that at our home-caring group that evening, I would ask for prayer.

But before I got around to sharing, a man came over and put his hand on my shoulder. "Monty, as we drove here tonight, the Lord impressed on me that I was to give you this verse. Maybe you'll understand it: 'The spirit of God is upon me because the Lord hath anointed me to preach good tidings unto the meek. He has sent me to bind up the broken-hearted, to proclaim liberty to the captives....' "

I hugged him. "Yes, Phil, I do know what it means. It means I have to quit my job."

20

Visions Brought to Life

Part One

Monty:

"Dad, snow!" announced Jared.

We were on the Bitterroot Pass summit, the western gateway to Montana. I pulled the pickup truck off the freeway. "Holly, let's show Jared how to make professional snowballs."

The Scripture given to me at the home-caring group was a confirmation of what God had told Holly and me. I had a responsibility to help the captives.

Although it was spring, a construction company's busiest time, Wilbur Vorhees graciously gave me a couple weeks off, and here we were, heading back to the place where I knew a lot of captives waited for pardon—the Montana prison.

The rushing traffic had left its mark on the roadside snow, making its once-clean slate dirty and unusable—the way life had left its mark on a boy named Monty Christensen. A boy, turned into Monty Montana, hightailing it across this same range of mountains in a Cadillac Eldorado, drugs and gun by his side.

Holly and Jared found a clean patch of snow, and Jared's well-aimed toss splayed the front of my jacket. I laughed and scooped up a handful of crisp, glistening powder, pretending I was going to wash someone's face. This light-hearted, free existence— could I get it across to prisoners that it could be theirs for the choosing? A choice of turning their backs on the former life-styles to follow Jesus—a choice to continue walking with Him although the enemy has knocked them flat. And that when they choose Him, He washes away the grime, making them like clean newborns? Could I make them understand? God, I don't know, I thought. The responsibility is awesome.

I dropped my offensive attack and threw my arms in front of my face to ward off a barrage of snowballs. "Just tell them, Monty," came a gentle voice inside me. "Tell the men what I have done for you, and let Me do the rest."

We pulled up to the same prison gate from which I had emerged a few months before. A sandpapery feeling started in my stomach as I retraced my steps past the guards with their rifles, past cell blocks where pruno was stashed, where throats were cut. A thought crossed my mind. Maybe my parole had been revoked, and once inside I'd never get out. For a fleeting moment I wanted to run.

"Monty Christensen?" The new chaplain came up to greet me. "The men are waiting to hear you."

I didn't preach. I shared the "agape-love" message. The kind of love I was learning from Pastor Rozell. I poured out my heart. The guys in there had never heard about agape. They had a lot of people telling them they were going to hell, but no one told them they were loved. And they responded. Twenty-three cons gave their hearts to Jesus.

After the service I went back to the pickup and climbed into the canopy-covered truck bed with Holly and Jared.

"Honey, we've gone through frustration and pain to be here, but now I know. This *is* God's plan."

I'm sure glad," came Holly's muffled reply as she scooted farther down in her sleeping bag, "because it's snowing, and I'm freezing, and I wouldn't want to be going through this if it weren't His plan."

Before we left Deer Lodge, I asked the chaplain about my former cellmate, John. I hadn't seen him in chapel. "He was part of our Over-the-Wall-in-the-Spirit Gang," I explained. "He led his entire family to the Lord."

"John had a minimum of eleven years on him," said the chaplain. "But he got out in nine months, right after you did. It was a miracle. He and his wife bought a Christian bookstore, and he's doing fine. Monty, please come back. You may share my pulpit anytime."

His comments put me in orbit. "We're launched into ministry; we're on the sawdust trail," I exulted to Holly during the seventeen-hour drive back to Bellevue. "I'm sure our county jail could use my services."

I called the jail chaplain and explained how the men in Montana had responded and that I'd like to work with him. I stood in disbelief as he spoke in my ear. "That's not possible. I don't allow guys like you to come in. I work here all year, and you guys come in to skim the cream off the top, and I get left with the hard work."

I hung up the phone and cried. The bottom had fallen out of my ministry. "He's right, God," I said. "I go in and they accept you, but then the wolves devour them because there's no one there to support them— to disciple them in Your ways. So what's the use?"

A few days later Holly opened the mail. "God knows what He's doing." She waved a letter at me. "It's a newsletter from the Prison Fellowship Ministry. The week after you were at the Montana prison, they went in for a four-day seminar on discipleship and are following up."

"Praise God," I said. "Then we're doing what we're supposed to. We have our ministry and another part of the Body of Christ has another. The fact that the door was closed to the local jail wasn't Satan trying to hinder the work. It meant that the Lord wants me to focus on prisons."

Holly gave me a kiss on the cheek. "When the Lord closes a door, He has an open door someplace else," she recited.

"So your husband's learning not to beat his head against the closed ones." I laughed and twirled her around for a super kiss. Jared giggled.

* * *

The Washington State Prison at Walla Walla. I was there with three other men from church whose credentials were impressive—two police officers and Tom, a former F.B.I. agent. The prison chaplain said, "Monty, I just learned that you're an ex-con. I feel strongly that you're to speak and spend as much time with the men as you like."

I was scared. My old Montana prison was one thing. This, something different. The Lord was pushing me out of the nest.

The chaplain invited me to come back the following week. "And bring your wife. She can talk to the wives."

After Holly and I had ministered, he said, "God is working through you. Move here, live with us, and work with the men on a daily basis."

Driving home, Holly and I agreed it was a tempting offer. We could be of service there, but what was God's desire? I decided that if He closed the doors to other prison work, we'd go to Walla Walla.

On our return, I contacted the chaplain of our area's large men's reformatory. I had heard he closely screened those who helped him with his work. This would be a good test.

"Monty," he said in response to my request to help, "I feel that your calling is of the Lord. I'll drive to Bellevue and meet you for lunch. I want you to be involved."

After a few times of sharing with the men in that prison, the chaplain submitted my name to receive a blue clearance badge that would be honored in every institution in the state. And it came through! I couldn't believe it—me, an ex-con, having free rein to walk the institutions from cell to cell and having access to chapel keys, without even being searched.

"This has never been done before, Monty," the chaplain said. He laughed. "And it probably won't happen again. God's got His hand on you."

An inmate said, "Whoa, Man, just seeing you be able to do this helps us."

I've received calls from the sergeant of the guards, saying, "Come down to 'lower max' and talk to this guy who says God told him to kill somebody."

I'd go, and also talk to the other men, and then go outside to my pickup and cry out to God to intervene in lives. "I know where they're at, Lord. I know how they hurt."

We've held many services at that reformatory, sometimes taking along singing groups, but the men say that seeing Holly and me there together, walking side by side with the Lord is the best ministry. "You two are a living miracle. There's hope for us."

* * *

"Monty Christensen?"

I opened my eye and squinted at the clock. Six in the morning. At that hour I wasn't sure who I was. "Yeah, I think so," I yawned.

"This is the 700 Club. We heard about your prison ministry and would like to come out to Washington and interview you. May I ask you a few questions?"

Suddenly I was awake. "Sure."

We spent an hour on the phone telling about our struggles and stumbles. There had been so many it sounded repetitious to our own ears. They might change their minds about interviewing.

But Bill Freeman and his camera crew came out and spent the day. We relaxed and forgot about the cameras as we walked and recreated scenes from our lives. Over pizza, Bill asked more questions.

"This prison ministry certainly is ordained of God," he said, as he left. He is still a firm friend.

After the program was aired, we received calls and letters from many areas asking how they could help or asking us to talk to them. The elders and deacons of our church invited me to a special meeting where they prayed over me and sent me, in the name of Jesus, to the prisons. "We are 100 percent behind you, Monty."

It turned out that these tremendous people have been 200 percent behind us in finances, opportunities, and open doors. Individuals with various expertise backgrounds offered their services to get our ministry organized and off the ground.

So, through pain and struggling, we were on our way. I think God's call on our lives is like a seed. It grows and breaks through hard ground. There's pain as the wind shakes the plant, but as the soil vibrates, the roots go deeper. Sometimes it's because of opposition and pain that a ministry is born. We had felt the birth pains and now, for the first time, were seeing life.

Part Two

Holly:

The evening at the home-caring group when Monty received confirmation of his ministry, Holly was excited. But now, pulling to a stop beside the Montana prison's gate, a lump of apprehension took root in her stomach.

She gazed at the dingy, high rock wall, remembering the embarrassing, scary days. She saw the other women with the hurt, beaten looks on their faces. She wanted to go home. This life didn't exist anymore.

Monty turned off the ignition and turned to her, concern on his face. "Sweetheart, I've got to go in and speak. What will you and Jared do?"

Holly started to shrug, but stopped as she remembered the woman at the bus stop the first day there. "You must be stayin' at Bill's—a kindly soul—lets wives and girlfriends stay free," she had said.

"Jared and I are going to pay a visit to Bill," Holly said with a decided nod.

She stood in front of the door of the plain, frame house. What was she doing here? Visions of being scrutinized by the women and hearing "Hotshot, huh?" flashed before her. What did she think she could do? Then she remembered Lamar's wife and resolutely knocked on the door.

"Hello, I'm Holly Christensen," she said to the woman who opened the door. "My husband, who used to be an inmate in the prison, is speaking to the men in the chapel tonight, and I thought I'd come by to see if there's anything I can do to help you."

The woman shifted her crying baby to her other hip and motioned Holly in. "You mus' be Monty's wife. My man said he's hearin' him tonight. Hey, Girls, Monty's wife and boy are here."

Women of all ages crowded around Holly and Jared.

"We heard about you."

Someone pushed a can of soda in Jared's hand, and the questions continued to flow.

"What's it like when your husband gets out?"

"Why don't you have a cup of coffee? Bill's gone to church tonight."

Holly looked around at the earnest faces, took a deep breath and said, "Well, when Monty got out, reality hit. We had a romance during his sentence. We'd write romantic letters and say romantic things when we were together."

"Uh-huh," several of the women agreed.

"But when he got out, it was a shock. We were together all the time, going through stuff all couples go through, but we didn't know how to be married. We had to learn...."

Before Holly knew it, it was time to go back to prison. As she and Jared drove away, Jared said, "Those ladies sure listened, Mom. They listened hard."

That night after Monty and Jared were asleep, Holly snuggled in her sleeping bag as the wind blew spring sleet against the truck windows. She thought, "Two years ago, if anyone had told me I'd experience what I've experienced tonight, I'd have told them they were nuts!"

* * *

1984

"You're pregnant," said the doctor, after he finished examining Holly.

"Good," she said. "I've wanted another baby so much. My husband wasn't with me for our first child, so this will be special."

Later she broke the news to Monty. "We'll attend classes in Lamaze. This will be wonderful."

"Finances will be tight, Holly. We're trying to get the nonprofit corporation set up, and I'm not working so much." He hugged her. "But the Lord will take care of us, baby and all."

A familiar, scared feeling settled around Holly's heart. "Well," she heard herself saying, "providing for our needs is more important than preaching."

Oh, no, she thought. Why did I say that? It was too late to retrieve the words, and she walked out of the room.

In a couple of weeks the third-notice bills hit. The heat was shut off, and the bank sent notice their car would be repossessed in ten days.

"This is like a roller-coaster ride," Holly stormed through her tears. "One minute you're working and the bills are paid, then disaster. This isn't the way we're supposed to live."

"I know," sighed Monty. He grabbed Holly's hand and pulled her to her knees beside him. "Lord, we're discouraged. We feel as though we've been misled, that You aren't in this ministry. Our faith is getting down to rock bottom, and we thank You for showing us what You want us to do. Amen."

He left to do some errands. Holly wiped her eyes and answered the ringing telephone.

"Hi," said her friend. "I'm coming by to take you out to the Carnation farms. I'd like to buy you some produce and dairy stuff."

When Holly returned, Monty waited for her, a sad look on his face. "I stopped at the post office to check on this certified-mail notice. I'm sorry, Honey; it's bad news." A smile spread over his face. "It's a check for one thousand dollars," he whooped, "from some people who want to support the ministry."

"Oh, no," Holly cried. "Look what the Lord did for us, and I...I didn't trust Him."

Monty put his arms around her. "Don't feel bad. I cried right there in the post office for the same reason." He laughed. "You'd think getting a thousand-dollar check would be a blessing, but in this case, it was chastisement. Our dear Father chastised us with blessing."

* * *

During the fourth month of pregnancy, Holly awakened Monty in the middle of the night. "Monty, the baby kicked for the first time. Isn't it wonderful?"

As she lay in bed, her hand on her abdomen, staring into the blackness, she thought, I've felt life before. With Jared, and with...with...She closed her eyes trying to squeeze away how it had felt, the first time she was pregnant.

"It's like a baby bird fluttering inside me," she had said in awe to a friend.

But it hadn't been a baby bird. It was a delicate little girl. And she had killed her. Holly silently shook her head on the pillow while tears streamed from the corners of her eyes.

The next morning she left for her part-time job. I won't think about the abortion, she said to herself. I'll keep so busy there won't be time to think until the baby is here. But each night in the silence, she cried.

* * *

The day she went into labor, the doctor said, "We're doing a C-section."

Does nothing turn out right? She panted as another contraction hit. Maybe this is punishment for the first baby. This baby will die, and that will be God's ultimate punishment.

She saw Monty's face in the anesthesia's murkiness. "Holly, we have a little boy. He's a go-getter. Are we still naming him Joshua?"

Holly nodded and tried to smile. Then she turned

261

her face to the wall.

When she brought Joshua home, she said to Monty, "We have two wonderful sons. I won't be depressed any more."

But the depression continued. "Postpartum and postsurgical blues," the doctor said. But it went deeper than that.

"Honey, how can I help you?" Monty's face was a combination of concern and helplessness.

"No way you can. The abortion act has been done, and I can't forgive myself. I don't think God really can, either. I murdered a helpless child!"

Monty took her hands in his. "Sweetheart, God despises abortion, but He loves you. You've asked His forgiveness for it. So have I. Remember, He forgives seventy times seven and beyond." He picked up the Bible and flipped pages.

Holly sank into a chair burying her head in her hands.

"Look," he said, "In Isaiah 43:25, 'I wipe out your transgressions....I will not remember your sins.' Honey, in Christ, there is no past. Everything is new. He doesn't want you dwelling on something that isn't there anymore. He wants you to have a victorious, happy life. The only thing you can do with the memory is to sometimes use it to help someone else."

Holly sat still, letting his words sink into her soul. Finally she raised her head. "You know, after the baby's death, I tried to ignore my emotions and forget about it. I never really grieved. I'm doing that now, and I'll be okay. What would I do without God or you?" Through the moistness obscuring her vision, she smiled.

* * *

"Holly Christensen? The reformatory chaplain told me to call you. Said you could help me. My husband's in for ten years. I don't know what to do."

"It's hard, I know," Holly said to the woman. "I couldn't have made it without Jesus."

"Religion? I didn't know that's what this was about. That's not my bag." The phone on the other end clicked.

Holly thoughtfully replaced her receiver. "Lord, whoever that was, someplace down the road, let her meet You." She turned to Monty. "It gets discouraging when wives are scattered all over the place, so it's impossible to get a Bible study or support group going, and also when I can't really share with people like that."

Monty looked up from the board game he was playing with Jared. "That is discouraging, Honey, but the Lord has annointed you right now for the job of childrearing. By the way, one of the guys at the prison hasn't heard from his wife for awhile. She's a Christian but got so discouraged with him, she's thinking about a divorce. He wondered if you would call her."

The next day on the phone, the wife said, "I feel like I'm going crazy. I've had it with my husband. He's back in jail after promising me....I just want to be free."

Holly replied, "I know how you're feeling. God had to deal with my resentment and bitterness. I had to learn that what I carried in my own heart wasn't any different from what Monty did."

The woman sputtered, "What do you mean?"

Holly smiled at the unseen, hurting wife. "Let me tell you how I had to learn to forgive. There's this thing called surrendering...."

Part Three

Monty:

"Listen, Friend, all the stuff you're sentenced for was done under the influence of booze. Face it, you're an alcoholic. Why don't you get counseling in that area, and then get into a support group. I am."

"You're in A.A.?" The inmate looked at me in amazement.

"Not exactly," I said. "It's a Christ-centered group. Man, I need it."

"Huh." He shook his head. "Guess if you need it, I sure do. Okay."

I watched him leave, thinking about the gruff guy who came to our church's alcohol meeting the night before. He was tattooed all the way to his fingertips. His front teeth were knocked out, and one finger was cut off. On the end of the stub was a tattooed smiley face. During the evening he gave his heart to the Lord. After the meeting, his neighbor, a little seventy-seven year old lady came to take him home.

"I've been praying for him for a long time," she said when she heard the news. "He had to come to his own decision."

Helping them make their own decisions is the only way I can counsel men in prison. When I'm with them in a one-on-one, I say up front, "I don't have your answers. You have. I will help you work through the distress, the frustration, the pain, the garbage that's piled on top of your answers. I'll help you clean it away and deal with it, but you'll have to come to your own decisions."

A good example of that is in a letter I came across recently. It's addressed "To an inmate," and part of it goes like this:

> Let's stop feeling sorry for ourselves and do something to improve our attitudes. Statistics show that the average level of education in this institution is half way through fifth grade. Ninety percent of our population suffered from malnutrition at the time of incarceration. That doesn't sound like arrest; that sounds like rescue.

Forget about the judge, the prosecutor, and parole board. God doesn't make mistakes. He has a reason for us to be here. We had best figure out what it is and take care of it. If we don't, we may have to make another trip to this wonderful place of opportunity. After a few trips we may get to liking it so well we won't ever want to leave. God doesn't want us living off the tax-payers forever. He wants us to be assets to the community, a contributor, people capable of helping others less fortunate than ourselves. To accomplish this will take less complaining, more work, and more prayer. Let's do it!

From an inmate

I, Monty Christensen, had to stop feeling sorry for myself, and with God's help, find my own answers. I have no other area of ministry, other than sharing that God forgives, heals, and gives strength to stick by decisions.

* * *

Churches across denominational lines began inviting me to speak. At first I didn't know what to say. After all, these were people who had grown up in the church, who wore three-piece suits, had doctorate degrees, and social standing. I had more trouble accepting them than I did the drunk on the street. I could identify with him. I was sure these people couldn't identify with me.

But God had been teaching me. He had put me in a church surrounded by these people, and while at times I was uncomfortable, He showed me that sometimes there's more bondage in church members than in the drunk, that people can make prisons of their own hearts. And He taught me to accept and love them, as He was teaching them to do the same to me.

So I counted the gallons of gas in my car and went. After telling them a little about my background, I told them how the church can help others like me.

"First we have to be like the Sunday School student, who, when asked to name the first prostitute that Jesus saw, answered, 'Jesus never saw prostitutes, He saw people.'"

Jesus doesn't look at what we are. He sees what we can become. We need people helpers who don't categorize, or pigeon-hole others—some clean and others unclean. When you see a dirty, long-haired kid in McDonald's or when a prostitute passes you on the street, can you use the Holy Spirit's power and see them complete and whole? If you can, you can see them through their growing pains. Life-style change takes time and you don't put high expectations on those who are crippled. You can be patient when twisted emotions are released for the first time, even when they emerge in a way that's not quite right. You can look beyond and see them whole and stable. Just remember that even after asking Jesus to forgive them, these broken people labor under guilt. Church, the strongest message today is 'You're forgiven.'"

* * *

1986:

"This is the first program of 'Today's Prison Epistle,' " I said, staring into the blank eye of the video camera. "Today we have as our guest an attorney who specializes in criminal cases."

Since that day, the video-tape outreach, under the auspices of The Neighborhood Church, has mushroomed. The local reformatory, the state prison, and others run the weekly program on their inside channels. On it I share my life and tap the skills and advice of professionals. It's a wonderful dilemma that the demand for the show exceeds my ability to produce.

One convict said recently, "Monty, I feel God will bless you and your family for your honesty. He will lift up your family."

I said, "Mac, you couldn't have known the extent to which we've been telling the truth about our lives."

Sharing my life hasn't been easy. The dirty wash is there for the world to see. But we're not responsible for what people think; we're only responsible for telling the truth. And as we do, life becomes more and more a blessing.

One afternoon, as I headed to an Alaskan prison, the chaplaincy co-ordinator said, "Sometimes we have only one or two inmates in the Bible study here, so don't be disappointed."

"If God wanted me to come this far for that many," I said, "it's fine. He's Boss."

The superintendant of the prison asked me why I was in Alaska. I told her, and I told her about Jesus.

"You and the chaplain join me for dinner," she commanded.

Although prison food isn't the height of my day, how could I refuse? I was halfway through dinner when she said to the guard sergeant, "Get on the intercom and have *all* the inmates return to the chow hall." She looked at me. "You finished yet, Christensen?"

"Sure am."

Standing up, she told the inmates, "We have a special guest from Washington State. Now listen up, because what he has to say isn't religious."

The chaplain's stunned look reflected my own shock. As I looked out over that congregation of men with cigarettes hanging from their mouths and exaggerated expressions of boredom on their faces, my heart seemed to race to catch up to itself, and my knees felt weak.

"Just tell them, Monty," came a familiar, loved voice within me. "Tell them about you and Me."

I took a deep breath, and said, "Men, I want to tell you about a guy. A guy named Monty Montana...."

✧ ✧ ✧

A PERSONAL NOTE

From Monty

In December 1986, I stood on a Seattle sidewalk, when a police car, siren screaming, screeched alongside. My heart seemed to turn upside down as the lights flashed in my eyes. I ran, but the police caught me, handcuffed me, and pushed me into the car. My shoulder-length hair fell over my eyes.

As they booked and fingerprinted me at the police department, I wondered, was this a dream? But it was real. The only differences between this incident and those of ten years before, were that this arrest was staged for a "Today's Prison Epistle" television program; the long hair was a wig; and I could go home when it was over.

But to those who can't go home, our Prison Impact Ministry continues to extend caring hands. To those who are in physical or spiritual bondage, we proclaim the freedom that Christ Jesus offers.

The video, truly God's invention, has allowed us to effectively communicate to men in prisons, by interviewing persons such as Bob Erler, the "Catch-Me-Killer," and Ron Rearick, the "Ice-Man," and Chaplain Ray. They and a host of other ex-cons level with the inmates about how to get off the roller coaster.

Our family, as well as the ministry, has expanded. Number three son, Shawn, was born in August 1986, and with God's grace, we expect another child in a few months. "Sons are a heritage from the Lord; children, a reward from Him" (Psa. 127:3 NIV).

Not long ago, my mother, stepfather and I had an occasion to really talk. I said, "God healed me from the wounds of my growing up years. And He wants to heal you both and remove from you the guilt of the failures of my life. I've forgiven you and God forgives you. You're free."

After that day, the Lord allowed a new relationship to form between my mother and me. I love her very much.

The original visions that God gave me are still fresh and new, and call to many others to be part of them. Our churches contain the resources, filled with the Living Water of Jesus, to carry to dry, parched, devastated lives.

We envision volunteer institution-chaplains. We envision expanding the video-ministry to national prison coverage. Taping interviews with inmates, and actual prison life, would show young peole the un-glamorous side of the criminal life. But for the fulfillment of these visions, we need workers, and then other workers to continue giving support as newly-changed lives grow to maturity.

When I speak in churches, I challenge people to get involved—to break Satan's stronghold in people's lives, and claim the victory for the Kingdom of God. The warfare is intense, but Holly and I are committed to seeing our Lord glorified, by bringing much fruit to Him. He is worthy of all our resources and efforts.

Until our Lord's return, Isaiah 61:1 will continue to impact my life.

> The Spirit of the Sovereign Lord is on me, because the Lord has anointed me to preach good news to the poor. He has sent me to bind up the brokenhearted, to proclaim freedom for the captives and release for the prisoners. (NIV)

A PERSONAL NOTE

From Holly

Not long ago I had the privilege of visiting the "Today's Prison Epistle" video studio as the camera crew and Monty were taping an interview with Madeline Manning Mims, former Olympic Gold-Medal winner. Thinking about all the people God has brought into our lives brought tears of joy.

I asked God why these people were so dedicated to helping us in this ministry. He quietly let me know that it was because it was His ministry to set free those who live in darkness. And the volunteers wanted to be a part of what He's doing.

Since that day in the studio, I've reflected over the years of devastation, and the years of blessing, and have felt overwhelmed at God's faithfulness. He has been so gracious to heal those broken times of our lives. It seems as if the past has never taken place. He has healed the wounds, only leaving a faint memory of the past. We can now recall the events, but outside an occasional twinge of regret, there is no pain.

I am excited about what God has planned for this ministry—that every aspect will bring His healing touch for many who are walking the same road we've traveled.

To appoint unto them that mourn in Zion, to give unto them beauty for ashes, the oil of joy for mourning, the garment of praise for the spirit of heaviness. (Isa. 61:3)